Data
Science

Learn About the Realms of Data Science From a-z

(Ultimate Guide to Master Data Mining and Data-analytic From Linear Algebra)

Timothy Cooper

Published By **Jordan Levy**

Timothy Cooper

Data Science: Learn About the Realms of Data Science From a-z (Ultimate Guide to Master Data Mining and Data-analytic From Linear Algebra)

ISBN   978-1-998901-35-7

No part of this guidebook shall be reproduced in any form without permission in writing from the publisher except in the case of brief quotations embodied in critical articles or reviews.

Legal & Disclaimer

The information contained in this ebook is not designed to replace or take the place of any form of medicine or professional medical advice. The information in this ebook has been provided for educational & entertainment purposes only.

The information contained in this book has been compiled from sources deemed reliable, and it is accurate to the best of the Author's knowledge; however, the Author cannot guarantee its accuracy and validity and cannot be held liable for any errors or omissions. Changes are periodically made to this book. You must consult your doctor or get professional medical advice before using any of the suggested remedies, techniques, or information in this book.

Table Of Contents

Chapter 1: What Is Data Science?

The first thing that we need to focus on is what data science is all about. Data science is going to be a very detailed study of the flow of information from a large amount of data that is presented to a company. In our modern world, there is information everywhere that we turn. Companies can set up their machines, their social media accounts and other social media products to collect an enormous amount of data from their customers. This data is much broader in scope than we will see with anything that has been done in the past.

While gathering all of this information may seem like a goldmine, the problem comes when we try to figure out what we are going to do with all of that data. It does not do us much good to hold onto that information, without any idea of what to do with it, or what is found inside. Because we have so much information present in this set, it is hard for a single person to go through and find the trends and the patterns that are in there by themselves.

Data science is here to handle this kind of problem. It is going to step in to help us figure out what is found in the information, and even how to store the information. With the help of artificial intelligence and machine learning, which we will talk about a bit later, we will find that data science will be able to go through the information and find what trends are there, especially the ones that are hidden.

When it comes to data science, we are going to be able to obtain some meaningful insights from raw and unstructured data, which is then going to be processed through skills that are business, programming, and analytical. Let's take a look at more about what this data science is all about, why it is important, and some of the different parts of the data science cycle.

The Importance of This Data Science

To start with, we need to figure out why this data science industry is so important. In a world that is turning more to the digital space than it ever did before, organizations are going to deal with a ton of data, data that is unstructured and structured, on a daily basis. Some of the evolving technologies that we can look at have enabled us to save a lot of money, and smart storage spaces have come up in order to store a lot of this data until companies can get to it.

Currently, there is a huge need for skilled and certified data scientists to help go through this information and see what is found inside. In fact, when it comes to the IT industry, these data scientists are going to be among the highest-paid professionals out there. According to Forbes, the annual salary for the average data scientist is almost $110,000.

Why is this industry paying so much? Because it is in high demand and many companies are looking to find qualified professionals who can gather, store, and look through all of the data that they have available and provide them with predictions, information, and help in using this information to make good business decisions. The number of professionals who are actually able to process and derive valuable insights out of the data is few and far between, so they are in high demand.

Furthermore, there are a lot of requirements out there in order to become a data scientist. Because of all this, there is going to be a 50 percent gap in the industry when it comes to the demand for data scientists versus the supply of these professionals. This is why it is so important to learn more about data science and how this kind of topic is changing up so many industries throughout our world.

With that in mind, we need to focus a bit more on data science and all of the different parts that are going to come with it. In the last few years, we have been able to see a large amount of growth in one field that is known as the Internet of Things (IoT). Because of this growth, we see that 90 percent of the data in our current world has been generated by and for this IoT field.

Each day, we see 25 quintillion bytes of data generated for companies to use, and this number will grow at an even faster rate as IoT continues to thrive. This extraordinary amount of growth in data can be useful for a lot of companies to learn about their customers, focusing on the best products to release next, and working toward the customer service they would like to provide. All of this data is going to come from a variety of sources that will include:

Sensors are set up in shopping malls in order to gather up the information of the individual shopper.

Posts on the various platforms of social media can send back information to the company.

Videos that are found on our phones and digital pictures are taking in more data than ever before.

Companies are able even to get some good information when they look at some of the purchase transactions that come when people shop online and through e-commerce.

All of this data, no matter its source, is known as big data. As you can imagine, with all of the various sources for information, companies are going to be flooded with more data than they know what to do with. It is impossible for an individual to go through and do all of the work on their own. This is why it is so important to really know what we should do with all of this data and the best way to utilize it in order to make good business decisions in the future.

It is here that the idea of data science is going to start showing up into the picture. Data science is going to bring together a ton of skills that we can find in the world of business, including business domain knowledge, mathematics, and statistics. All of these are important because they are going to help an organization out in a variety of ways, including:

Helping the company learn new ways where they can reduce costs each day.

It can help the company figure out the best method to take to get into a new market that will be profitable for them.

This can help the company learn about a variety of demographics and how to tap into these

It can help the company to take a look at the marketing campaign that they sent out there and then figure out if the marketing campaign was actually effective.

It can make it easier for the company to launch a new service or product successfully.

These are just a few aspects of business that this big data is going to be able to help us out with. This means that no matter what kind of industry will be able to use the ideas of data science in order to help them learn about their customers, their marketing campaigns, their products and more and lead up to more success for the company.

How Some Top Industry Leaders Use Data Science

In this section we are going to take a look at some data science can actually be used, and how some of the industry leaders, such as Amazon and Google, are already using data science in order to help them get ahead of the competition in many different areas. IT organizations have a big need in order to address some of their expanding and complex data environments to help them identify some new sources of value, exploit the opportunities that are there, or find ways to optimize and grow themselves in an efficient manner.

Here, one of the biggest deciding factors for the organization is what value they are going to be able to extract from their data repository using analytics, and how well they can present this information. Let's look at some examples of the big leaders of the industry and how they are using data science, and data scientists, to help get things done.

First on the list is Google. Google is going to be the biggest company that is hiring data scientists right now. This is because a lot of the products that Google is releasing right now, and a lot of the features that they are offering to their customers are drive-by data science, especially artificial intelligence, and machine learning.

Amazon is another good example of how we can work with this. Amazon is seen as a global e-commerce and cloud computing giant that is also working on lots of projects in the data science world and hiring data scientists all the time. They need these professionals to help them learn more about their customers and the needs of these customers while enhancing the geographical reach of both their cloud domains and e-commerce domains as well, along with some of the other goals they have to drive business.

And we can also look at Visa and see how they are working with data science as well. Visa is known as an online financial gateway for a lot of companies, and in one day, they can do transactions that are worth hundreds of millions. Due to this fact, the need for qualified and professional data scientists is high at this company so that they can keep customers and companies safe, and generate even more revenue in the process, check out transactions that could be fraudulent, and customize some of the services and products based on the requirements of the customer.

The Life Cycle of Data Science

The next thing that we are going to take a look at here that can be kind of fun is the idea of the data science life cycle. For a better understanding of how this whole process of data science is going to work, we need to actually look at what is known as the life cycle of this data science, and how it is going to influence a lot of different things for the business.

To start, let's say that we have a Mr. X and he owns a retail store. His whole goal here is to help improve the sales that his store sees by identifying the main drivers of those sales. To help Mr. X accomplish this new goal, he has a few questions that he needs to answer, and these are going to include:

Which products in the store are going to bring him the most profit on a regular basis?

How are some of the promotions that he is doing in-store working at making sales?

Are the different placements of products that are used in-store deployed in an effective manner?

The primary aim that we are going for here is to answer these questions, which is really going to have a lot of influence on the project and the outcome that it has. Because of this, Mr. X decides to hire on a data scientist to sort through all of the data that is available and determine the right course of action along the way. Let's use the life cycle of data science, which we are going to discuss below, to help us to solve this problem and see how the owner can do to improve sales and revenues.

Data Discovery

The first part of this data life cycle is known as data discovery. This part is going to include all of the ways that someone is able to discover data from a variety of sources. The data can come in many different forms, including in a format that is unstructured, such as in images or videos. But it can also come in a more structured format that would include files of text. There is also the possibility that it can come from a relational database system as well.

Right now, organizations are also able to take this a step further and are using social media to their advantage. It is not uncommon for a business to look at data they can obtain from social media, and other similar sources to help them to understand some of the mindset of their customers better than ever before. It is during this stage that the object is to take a look at some of the data that has been collected, and then figure out the best course of action to boost sales. Some of the things that we may see in this stage that are affecting sales for this business will include:

Store location

The locations and the promotions that competitors on the market are offering.

Product pricing

Product placement

Promotions

The hours that the business is open.

The staff and their knowledge about the products.

Keeping these factors in mind, we can develop a bit more clarity on the data, and it takes some time to help us actually find the data that we need. When we are all done with this stage, we can collect the data, from all of the different sources, especially any that are going to work with the elements that we have listed above, and then can move on to the second stage.

Data Preparation

Once we are done going through and discovering the data and finding it from all of the different sources that we can collect it from the second stage is going to include preparing the data. There is quite a bit that will go on in this stage, including converting the disparate data into a format that is common (if you have some text and some images, you need them to all be the same time to finish this process), so they all work together.

This part of the process is going to involve collecting data that is clean and then inserting the defaults where necessary, the ones that are suitable. In some cases, based on the kind of data you are working with, it could involve methods that are more complex, such as identifying some of the missing values through the process of modeling.

Once the cleaning of the data is done, the next step is to start integrating that data and then seeing if you can create your own conclusion from the set of data for analysis. This is going to involve the integration of data, which means that we need to merge two, and sometimes more, tables of the same objects, but storing different information, or it could mean summarizing fields in a table using aggregation. Basically, our goal here is to have a chance to explore, and even understand what values and patterns are hidden in all of this data so we can use it later.

 Mathematical Models

We also need to learn about some of the mathematical models that are found in our projects of data science, and how these models are there to drive our products. These models are going to be planned out ahead of time and built by data professionals so that they can suit the needs that are specific to the business. This could include a lot of different things depending on what the business needs the most, but some of the areas that could be included are logistics, linear regressions, statistics, differential and integral calculus and more.

There are a variety of tools and options that you can use when it comes to working on these mathematical models but setting them up in the proper manner is going to ensure that we actually can work on the data and learn what is inside. In some cases, you can also do fine with just one model, but depending on the complexity of the model and what your end goal is all about, it is possible that you will need to work with more than one model.

If more than one model is needed, the data scientist is going to spend some time creating a unique group of models.

After they have been able to measure out the models, the professional can then make any necessary revisions to the parameters and then fine-tune them for the next run with modeling. This could include a few different steps in order to get the work done, based on how long it takes until the professionals know they are working with the very best model for the job.

During this step, the data scientist is going to build up the mathematical models that they need, based on what the business really wants. This could be something like figuring out which product between two or three is the most profitable, whether the store is seeing success with their product placement, and so on. The success of the model, and whether or not it is working, often depends on what we are trying to monitor in the process.

Getting Things Going

Once we have taken the time to prepare the data the right way, and we have built up the models that we need to use, it is time for us to move on and get the models working. These models do us no good in theory; we have actually to put them to work to get the right results. There might be a lot of discrepancies along the way, and sometimes troubleshooting is going to be needed, and this is why a data scientist will need to tweak their models a few times before they get the most accurate results. In this stage, we are going to work to gather information and then derive the right outcomes based on the business requirements that are necessary at that time

Communication

This is going to be our final step, but don't think that this makes the step any less important or that you can skip over it any time that you would like. In this step, you need to be able to communicate the findings that came out of the data and out of your model. The data scientist will be the liaison between various teams, and if they are successful, they need to be able to seamlessly communicate the findings they got in the other steps to the key stakeholders and decision-makers in the organization. This helps to get actions taken based on that data, as well as based on the recommendations that the data scientist is going to give out at this time.

If we are still working with Mr. X from the retail store before, you could take the information that you found through the other steps, and then communicate and recommend certain changes to the business strategy that will help Mr. X to make necessary changes. If the work was done in the proper manner, your recommendations would read the data in the proper manner, and Mr. X - after implementing those recommendations - will be able to earn the maximum amount of profit.

The Components of Data Science

In this part of our discussion, we need to get a look at some of the different components that come with data science. There are actually quite a few that need to come together and work in order to get the most out of data science fully. The first component that comes with data science is going to be the various types of data. The raw set of data is going to be the foundation of our data science journey, and it can be found in various different types. The two main types will include structured data, which is often going to come in tabular form, and then the other one is going to be the unstructured data, which is going to include PDF files, emails, videos, and images.

The second component that we are going to find when we look at data science is programming. You have to come up with some programming in order to make those mathematical models that we talked about earlier and to get them to really sort through the information and make predictions. All of the analysis and management of the data is going to be done by computer programming. The two most popular languages that are used in data science will include R and Python, so learning one of these can be helpful.

Next on the list: probability and statistics. Data is going to be manipulated in a manner that it is able to extract information and trends out of that data. Probability and statistics are going to be the mathematical foundation that brings it all together. Without having a good idea and a lot of knowledge about these two topics, it is possible that you will misinterpret the data, and will come up with conclusions that are not correct. This is a big reason why probability and statistics are going to be so important to the world of data science.

We also have to take a look at the idea of machine learning when we are looking at data science. When someone is working through all of that big data and everything that is contained inside of it, they are also going to use a lot of the algorithms that come with machine learning. This can include the methods of classification and regression at the same time.

Someone who wants to work as a data scientist has to have a deep understanding of machine learning and a lot of the different algorithms that come with this kind of learning. Otherwise, they are going to misinterpret the data they have and can run into some problems. Machine learning is so important to this kind of field because it helps to take all of that available data, and the set of data is often quite large and can help them to make predictions and learn valuable insights in the process.

And finally, another key component that comes with this data science is big data. In our modern world, raw data is something that we can compare to crude oil. When we look at the way we extract refined oil from the crude oil, by using data science, we can extract useful and helpful information from our raw data. Some of the different tools that are already available for this that can help us process some of the big data will include Apache Spark, R. Pig, Hadoop, and Java, to name a few.

Many companies have become efficient at gathering large amounts of data about their stores, about their products, and about their customers. But because they are so efficient at gathering this information up, they now have so much of it that the process of diving in and sorting through all of it seems intense, and no one person can do it on their own. Even if a team tried to go through that information, it would take too long, and important information and trends that are needed to make smart decisions would be left behind and missed in the process.

This is where the idea of data science can come in. With the help of the right algorithms and more, the data scientist is able to sort through all of the big data and can find some of the big trends that are hidden inside. Often this is done in a manner of minutes, and maybe hours if there is a ton of data, through machine learning algorithms in the process.

These algorithms are quick and efficient and can provide the business owner with the tools and information they need to make sound business decisions in no time. For many companies, this is the method they are going to use in order to learn more about their customers, increase their sales, and gain an edge over the competition.

Chapter 2: What Exactly Does A Data Scientist Do?

The world - when it comes to data science and big data - can sometimes seem really complex when we are on the outside looking in. IN business, there are a lot of people who already know what the big data analysis is all about, and that it involves someone going in and collecting the ever-growing about of data that is being generated all of the time, and then using this information to come up with insights that are meaningful and will help the business to grow. But what this is going to involve in terms of the day to day job of the data scientist is a completely different thing to consider.

We are going to spend some time in this chapter looking at some of the things that the data scientist is going to do on a day to day basis, and what their job really entails. This can help us to understand why they are in such high demand overall, and why their job is so important to so many different companies right now.

Some of the Key Capabilities of a Data Scientist

The term data scientist is able to cover up many roles through a variety of organizations and industries, whether we are looking at the government, at finance, or even in academia. While there are a lot of capabilities that need to come into play, there are going to be three main ones that everyone who works as a data scientist has to be able to understand before they get started.

First, the data scientist has to understand that all of the data has some meaning. Often, we are going to overlook the fact that we have all of this data, and it actually means something, and it is important for us to understand what that meaning is all about. We have to be able to look beyond the numbers that are there, and then get a better understanding of what these numbers stand for. Without this understanding, then we are not going to be able to gain the insights that we need. Understanding the data that is presented to us is more of an art, and it is so important. All of the rest will not make sense or help you that much if you aren't able to understand the meaning of the data.

The next thing that a data scientist has to keep in mind is that they need to understand the problem that has to be solved, and how the data relates to and will be able to help out with that. Here we are going to spend some time opening up the tool kit to find the right analytics and approaches and algorithms that you can use in order to work with that data. There are literally hundreds of different techniques that you can use in order to get the data to solve your problems.

There are a lot of options to choose from out of your tool kit, and you have to pick out the right one. You can work with decision theory, control theory, game theory, and operations research, for example, and all of these have been around for a long time. Once we have had a chance to understand the data, and we understand what kind of problem we want to solve with that data, then it is possible to pick out the right tool, or the right algorithm, and get the solutions we want.

And finally, a data scientist has to have some kind of understanding of engineering. This is not really about understanding and then delivering the infrastructure that was required to perform these analyses. It isn't going to do us much good to solve the problem if we haven't first gone through and created the infrastructure to deliver the solutions in an effective manner, in an accurate manner, and at the right place and time.

Being a data scientist who can do their job correctly is going to be more about paying attention to all three of these capabilities. You have to pay attention to the kind of data you have and where it is coming from, along with what it all means. You need to understand the problems that should be solved, and know-how the different algorithms with machine learning can fit in with this. You have to have good knowledge when it comes to engineering so that you can come up with the right solutions to the problem.

We also have to remember with this one that all of this does not mean we have to kick out the idea of specialization. It is important to note that it is virtually impossible for someone to be an expert in all three of these areas, plus all of the little sub-areas that come with each of them. You should have some general knowledge when you work in this field but being an expert in all of them is going to be pretty much impossible.

This opens up the door for someone to specialize in one of the areas. As long as you also hold onto an appreciation for all three of them, you are going to be just fine and can do well in this field. For example, even though you could primarily be the engineer or the person who works with the algorithms, if you do not have a good understanding of all the parts, and you can't figure out the problem you want to solve, or what the data is, then you will make decisions that are bad and not smart for the business.

Some of the Key Qualities That Show Up in a Data Scientist

In terms of some of the personal qualities that come with this kind of professional, we need to start out with a sense of curiosity. You have to be curious about what the data is going to tell you, and how you can use that information to solve problems. Communication skills are going to be another critical component, as well. Data scientists have to spend a lot of their time talking to other people, such as the customers so that they can figure out what the problem is that they should solve, or even talking to vendors of data to find out what they can provide. This puts the data scientist into the position of being the middleman, and this means that communication is going to be so important.

There are a ton of different personality types that decide it is a good idea to go into data science, so each one you are going to meet will do things in their own way. This is part of what makes this field so exciting and will ensure that those who get into this field can remain an asset to the company, while still enjoying a lot of the work that they are doing in the process.

With this in mind, we need to take a look at some of the simple terms; a data scientist is going to help a company analyze the data for actionable insights. Some of the specific tasks that can be done with the help of a data scientist will include:

They are responsible for identifying some of the data analytics problems that are going to be used in the proper manner, offer some of the greatest opportunities to the organization.

They are going to be responsible for determining the correct sets of data and the variables that need to be used.

They are responsible for helping a business collect a ton of data, both the unstructured and the structured kind, from a large variety of sources to use in decision making.

They are responsible for cleaning and validating the data that they can find in order to make sure that the data is accurate that the data is complete (at least as much as possible), and that there is uniformity in the data as well.

They are responsible for devising and then applying various algorithms and models to mine the stores of big data that they helped to collect in the first place.

They are going to be responsible for analyzing the data to identify patterns and trends.

They will be able to interpret the data in order to discover the solutions and the opportunities that are there and will help the company to succeed the most.

They are responsible for being able to communicate any of the findings that they got with that big data. This information is going to be shown to the stakeholders with the help of visualization tools and any other means necessary.

To help us see the general view of this data scientist, we can look at them as a professional who knows how to extract the meaning from and also interprets the data that they have. This is going to require them to use both tools and methods that come to them from machine learning and statistics, along with some common sense. This person is going to spend a lot of their day collecting, cleaning, and then munging the data they have. This process is going to take in a lot of persistence overall, along with skills in statistics and engineering to get it all done. The data scientist must also contain the skills for understanding some of the biases in the data, and for debugging logging output from the code.

Once the data scientist has been able to get that data into shape, they will then do an analysis of the data that is more exploratory. This is going to be done with the help of data sense and visualization. The professional is going to find any patterns that are there, build up models, and work with the algorithms. This is sometimes done with the intention of understanding the usage of a product and the overall health of how the product is doing. Sometimes the information will serve as a prototype that will be put in with the product at some point.

In some cases, this professional is going to design their own experiments, and they will be critical when it comes to some of the decision making that is driven by data. They can also communicate with a lot of other people in the company, including the leadership, engineers, and other team members using data visualizations and clear language to make sure that everyone is on the same page and understands what is going on in that data.

What do I need in order to start with this career choice?

If you have been reading through this guidebook so far, it is likely that you are curious about what all it takes to become a data scientist and add this as your own career choice. Some of the things to look at to help determine if this is the right kind of career path for you will include:

Do you have, or are you willing to work towards, a degree in something like marketing, management information systems, computer science, statistics, and mathematics?

Do you have a lot of work experience in these kinds of areas?

Do you already find the idea of collecting and analyzing data interests you?

Do you like to do work that is more individualized and enjoy spending time problem-solving?

Are you able to do well with communicating with a lot of different people, both in a visual manner and verbally?

Would you like to find some methods that help broaden out your skills and do you enjoy taking on new challenges?

If you were able to answer yes to most of these questions, then you may find that the field of data science is going to be the right one for you. It takes a sharp and critical mind, as well as someone who is really curious and likes to find the answers that they need within the information.

Data scientists must have a good amount of knowledge in statistics and math, in addition to the information that we talked about above. A lot of the work that you do with your algorithms and other parts of data science is going to include these two things.

Another thing that you need is a natural curiosity, along with critical and creative thinking to go along with it. You have to be willing to look at the data and think about all of the things that you can do with the data. What undiscovered opportunities lie hidden within? Most of these professionals are good at connecting the dots, and they have a big desire to search out the answers to questions that have not yet been asked so that they can find the full potential that comes with the data.

An advanced degree for this kind of work is also pretty common. These professionals are going to have higher degrees than a lot of the fields out there, with about 88 percent of them having a master's degree as a minimum, and 46 percent have a Ph.D. This helps to ensure that they have the right knowledge and experience necessary in order to handle some of the complexities that come with their job.

During your education, it is often best to have a background that includes some computer programming. Since you need to use programming to help make up the algorithms and models for mining all of that big data, many languages can work for this. Understanding the basics of Python will make a big difference since this is the one that is most commonly used.

Some data scientists are also like entrepreneurs. Business strategy is important, whether you are an individual doing the work or you work on a team with other data scientists along the way. It is hard for you to be successful in this kind of career, or for any other professional to take off in it, if you are not able to first devise some of your own methods and build up your own infrastructures to slice and dice the data in a way that can help you find out new things, and figure out the new visions or the future out of all the data you have collected.

And the final part of the puzzle that is nice for a data scientist to have is good communication skills. These professionals have to spend a lot of time talking about the complex ideas they have and sharing these with people who need to know the information, but who are not well-versed in data science. This means that in this capacity, you need to take some of the complex topics that you are working on and explain them in a way that others will be able to understand as well.

There are several methods that you can utilize that will make this easier, such as data visualization tools. But your verbal communication skills need to be strong as well so that you can clearly tell the right story and make it easy for others to understand what you are doing with your work, and how this kind of data science is going to be beneficial to your needs.

The work of a data scientist can be complex. While it may seem like they just have to sort through some data and then are done for the week, there are a lot of different parts that have to come into the mix in order for these professionals to do their job properly. They need to know how to gather the data. They need to know how to clean the data and write out algorithms and models that will help them go through the data and find good trends and patterns that can make predictions. They need to be able to communicate in a clear and concise manner so that others can understand what these findings mean to them.

Chapter 3: A Look At What Data Analytics Is All About

While we are on the topic of data science, it is also important to take a look at data analytics. This is going to be a subset of our data science that we talked about earlier, and it is going to be important when it comes to handling the data that we can gather, from various sources, and then figuring out what it all means. You can hold onto all of the data that you want, but if you don't understand what that data is trying to tell you, then the data is pretty much worthless to you and your company. This is where the process of data analytics is going to come into play.

To start, data analytics is going to be the science of taking raw data and analyzing it in order to make some conclusions about that information. Many of the processes and the techniques that reused with this have been automated into algorithms and mechanical processes that will work over the raw data and turn it into something that humans can read through and understand.

When the techniques are used in the proper way, data analytics will help us to see trends and metrics that would be lost in other situations, lost in all of the data that you are holding onto. This information is then going to be used to help optimize processes to help increase how efficient a system or a business can be overall.

Now that we know a bit about the broad meaning of data analytics, it is time to get into some of the different parts of it, and how we can use it to our advantage. The term data analytics is going to be broad, and it includes many diverse types of data analysis. Any type of information that can be subjected to techniques of data analytics to get inside that can then be used by humans to improve something about their business will fall under this umbrella.

Let's look at an example of this. Many manufacturing companies are going to spend time recording the work queue, downtime and run time for the different machines that they are working with. They will then take the data that contains this information and use it to better plan how and when the workloads should happen. This helps the machines get as close to their peak capacity as possible, saving time and money in the process.

This is just one of the tasks that data analytics is going to be able to help out with, even though preventing bottlenecks in production is a good thing to pay attention to. Gaming companies are going to be able to use this process in order to set up the right reward schedules for players which is done in a way that ensures the majority of players stay active in the game rather than dropping off and rarely using it. Another example is a content company. They can use the various parts of data analytics in order to keep their customers clicking, watching or even reorganizing the content so that they can get the clicks and the views that they need.

We have to remember that data analysis is a complex process, and not one that you can just glance at and come up with the answers. If you do this, then it is likely that you are missing out on a lot of important information within that large set of data. Some of the steps that you can use in order to conduct a proper data analysis will include:

We start out this process by determining the requirements of the data, or how the data has been grouped together. There are a lot of possibilities here including the data being separated out by things like gender, income, demographics, and age. The values of the data could also be numerical, or they may be divided up by category as well.

Then in the second step of this is the process of collecting our data. There are a ton of different sources where you can get all of this information. It could be from your employees, from sources in the environment, online sources like surveys and social media, and even from your computer system.

Once the data has been collected, and you are sure you have the data that you need, it is time to organize the data Since you are collecting it from a variety of sources, you have to make sure that it is organized in a manner that makes sense, and one that the algorithm will be able to read through quickly and find the trends to make predictions from when you get to that step.

You can choose what method you would like to use when you organize the information. You can work with a spreadsheet or try some kind of software that is good at handling data that is statistical.

Once you have been able to organize the data the way that you would like, it is time to clean it all up before the analysis happens. This means that the data scientist has to go through and scrub the data and check that there are no errors or duplications that are found in the information, or that the data is not incomplete. This step takes some time, but it ensures that everything is fixed and ready to go before you even start.

The key points to remember from this part is that the data analytics is going to be the science of taking your raw data and then analyzing it to help make conclusions based on that information. The processes and techniques that are used with this have already been automated in many cases, and you will see this in use with algorithms that can take the raw data and make it work for human consumption. The main reason that a business would want to use this kind of process, and to analyze the data they have, is because these analytics are going to help the business to optimize their customer service to others and optimize their performance.

Why Does this Analysis Matter?

With this in mind, you probably already understand a little bit about why the process of data analytics is so important, and why a business would want to get this done with all of the information that they have gathered. They can use the information that is in the data, but often there is just so much data, and it comes from so many different locations, that it needs a bit of work in order to really see what is there, and to use it to make accurate predictions along the way based on the data.

The process of data analytics is going to be important because it is going to really help any kind of business that uses it to optimize their performances implementing it into the business model means that a company will be able to reduce their costs, simply by having the process identify more efficient ways for them to do business, and because it can help them to store in an efficient manner large amounts of data.

In addition to all of this, a company is going to be able to use the process of data analytics to make decisions that are so much better for their company. This analysis is also one of the best ways to analyze customer trends, and customer satisfaction, which is going to make it easier for the business to offer new and much better, products and services than they would without this kind of analysis happening.

The Different Types of Data Analysis

While we may look at this and assume all of the analysis is going to be the same, and that there isn't any variation that will show up, this is just not true. There are a few types of analysis that you can work with based on what you want to see happen in the end, and what your goal is when you work through the data. The four basic types of data analytics that most data scientists are going to work with include:

Descriptive analytics. This is one that will take the time to describe what has happened in the data over a chosen period of time. You may look at things like whether the number of views has gone up, or if the sales for your company are higher or lower than they were in the previous month for a product.

Diagnostic analytics This is the one that will focus more on why something has happened, or the root of how your business is doing. This one is helpful, but it will involve data inputs that are more diverse and a bit of hypothesizing in the process. For example, did you have a slow sales week because the weather was bad, and no one went out shopping? Or did something go wrong with one of your marketing campaigns and that is why sales are struggling?

Predictive analytics. This one is going to be used to help predict what is most likely to happen in the near future, based on the information that we have at our disposal right now. What happened to the sales last year when the summer was warm? How many weather models are going to tell us that there will be a hot summer this year, and we should prepare for more of what we saw in the past.

Prescriptive analytics. This one is going to be responsible for suggesting a course of action that the company should take. For example, if the likelihood of a hot summer is measured as an average of five weather models and this likelihood is above 58 percent, then it is likely that you should add in more shifts to handle the sales if this is something that has happened in the past.

When we use data analytics, it is going to underpin many of the quality control systems that are found in the financial world, and other companies as well. An example includes the program of Six Sigma that has taken over helping to reduce waste and increase creativity and efficiency. If you are not able to measure something properly, whether it's your own weight or the number of defects that you are getting per million during the line of production, then it is hard to optimize the work that you are doing.

Every business wants to optimize things, and they want to make sure that they are getting the most out of all the work they do along the way. Data analytics is one of the best ways to make this happen. It helps the company to really see what they can do, and ensures that they actually have some data, some hard facts behind all of their decisions before they even start.

Data analytics, as we discussed a bit before, is going to be a field that spends its time analyzing sets of data that the company has been able to gather from a variety of sources. When this analysis is done, we can then draw some conclusions from the information that was provided. It is a very popular strategy that is growing, and more industries over time are starting to jump on board and use it, from the healthcare field to the financial field and every industry in between.

Data scientists are going to spend a lot of time challenging themselves to not just draw a conclusion from the numbers they see but they also need to find the most efficient and useful way to analyze and use the information. This has to be done quickly. If it takes the data scientist five years to go through the data, then their work is not worth it. Trends change quickly, and there will be many more sets of data that come in during that time. The analysis must be done quickly, hopefully at a rate that is able to keep up with all of the data that keeps coming in during this time.

As the ways that we can gather up and store our information changes, companies need employees who not only can take a look at the data, but who can also keep themselves up to date on the most current methods of handling these numbers so the company can get the most use out of that information. The data scientist will also need to be able to keep a good eye on this information for future needs.

This is a lot of work and is not always as easy as it seems. The demand to handle all of this data and perform accurate and timely analysis on that information is going higher and higher, and the supply of professionals who can do this kind of work is not able to keep up. This is true in almost any field that is looking for a data scientist right now. Organizations are leveraging and analyzing an extraordinary amount of data, much more than they were ever able to do before. They want to continue doing this because it helps them to make decisions that are smart and driven by data, but it is something that takes a professional to do, and this can be a challenge to find the employees who will be able to handle the work for them.

The Benefits of Doing an Analysis of the Data

When it comes to performing a data analysis, there are a ton of benefits that any company, no matter what industry they are in, can receive from this process. It may seem like a long and drawn-out process that is hard to work with, and many companies fall into the habit of just collecting the data and then have no idea what they should do with it. But actually, analyzing the data that you have, and seeing what is inside can benefit your company in many different ways. Some of the best benefits that your company can receive from completing a data analysis will include:

Helps you to understand your customers better. All businesses want to understand their customers. This is the best way to make more sales and increase revenue. But how are you supposed to know what the customer wants, and what is going to convince them to come to your store compared to going over to a competitor? This data analysis can take information from customer surveys and customer habits and help you make more informed decisions to provide better customer service to increase sales as well.

Helps you to know what trends are going on that you should follow for your business. There are always trends that go on in any market, but these trends are often shifting and changing at really fast rates that are hard to keep up with. Using a data analysis can help you to catch on to some of the trends ahead of time, making it easier for you to really meet the needs of your customers.

It helps you to know your product better. Sometimes, this data analysis can be used to help you know which products are doing the best and why. You may find out that one product is actually doing better than you thought, or that you should start selling more of a similar product to increase sales.

It can help make smarter business decisions overall. It is always best if you can have data and information behind all of the decisions that you make for your company. The data analysis helps you to comb through all of that information and see what is there before you make any decisions about your company.

It is great for beating out the competition. Companies who are willing to take a look through all of that data, and see what trends are hidden inside are the ones to catch on to new information faster and can beat out others in the industry.

These benefits can help us to really see how important this data analysis can be for the whole company, and why it is in such high demand in almost every industry that is out there. For some smaller companies who are not choosing to gather as much data, and can work on a more local level, it may be too time and cost consuming. But for larger companies that need to work against a lot of competition, and who are juggling a lot of different parts, this can be the best option to help you get started with helping your business grow in more ways than one.

Who is using data analytics?

Another topic that we can explore is the idea of who is using data analytics already. The number of companies who can use this kind of process, and who are seeing a lot of benefits with this kind of process may surprise you. To start, you will find that the hospitality and travel industries are going to use this data analytics. Turnarounds for this industry are quick, and with data analysis, they can collect a lot of data from their customers and learn where the problems are. When the problems are found, it is easier for them to make changes that result in better service for everyone.

Healthcare is another industry that is using these ideas. Healthcare is able to combine the use of high volumes of data, whether this is structured or unstructured data, and then will use the process of data analytics to help the companies make decisions quickly. This could make a huge difference for many of the patients who utilize this system on a regular basis.

Even retailers can use data analysis. Think about all of the information that a retailer is able to collect from their customers over time, and when they use the information properly, they can meet the always-changing demands of their shoppers. The information that is collected by these retailers and then analyzed is going to help them to see what trends there are, can make better recommendations, and all comes together to increase the profits that are seen by the company.

Data analytics is going to be important no matter what kind of industry you are in at the time though. The examples above are just a start to the list, and any company or industry that collects data from social media, their customers, or from other sources, will need to do some kind of analysis on that data to see what is inside. It is so beneficial to many companies to do this, and skipping out on it, or thinking that it is not that important can really cause harm to your company.

Inside this information, you can learn what your customers want, what the complaints are and how you can fix them, what products to release to your customers, how to beat out the competition, what others are doing and so much more. Deciding not to look through this information, and ignoring all that it has to say is going to be a big mistake, and could leave you behind as your competition takes the lead simply because they knew it was important to do a data analysis ahead of time.

Chapter 4: What Is Data Mining And How Does It Fit In With Data Science?

Another topic that is important for us to spend some time discussing when it comes to data science is the idea of data mining. Data mining is going to be a process that is used by many companies in order to take some of the raw data that they have, and then turn it into information that is actually useful for them to use. By using the software, and a few other tools along the way, that can help them to look for patterns in all of the data they have collected, a business is able to learn a lot more about their customers.

So, why would a business want to learn all of this extra information about their customers? When the business does data mining properly, they will be able to develop marketing strategies that are more effective, can help to decrease their own costs, and even increase sales at the same time. Data mining is going to depend on the effective collection of data, along with computer processing and warehousing to get it all done.

One thing to note here is that the processes of data mining are going to be used to help us build up machine learning models. These models that rely on machine learning can power up applications, including the recommendation programs found on many websites, and the technology that is able to keep search engines running.

Some of the History That Comes with Data Mining

The process of going through all of the data that we have and trying to find some of the hidden connections that are there so that we can predict some of the future trends is actually something that has been around for a long time. While this is sometimes known as "knowledge discovery in databases," the term of data mining is not going to be something we heard about until the 1990s. But the foundations that come with it are going to have three different disciplines of science that are going to be intertwined with one another. These three points are going to include:

Statistics: This is going to be the numeric study of the relationship that is found in the data you are using.

Artificial intelligence: This is going to be the human-like intelligence that a machine or a type of software is able to exhibit when the right kind of coding is done.

Machine learning: These are the different algorithms that you can use on the data in order to have that data reveal its trends and help you make some predictions.

What was once an older topic is now newer again, as the technology that comes with data mining is evolving, even more, to help keep pace with all of the potential of big data, and thanks to the idea that computing power is becoming more affordable.

Over the past ten years or so, some of the advances that have happened in the speed and power of processing have made it easier to move beyond the time-consuming, tedious, and manual practices. We can instead work with a type of data analysis that is automated, easy, and quick. The more complex sets of data that we can collect, the more potential there is for data mining to find some really great insights that can help with the growth of your company.

You will find that there are a lot of companies that are going to work with data mining to discover the right relationships between demographics, promotions, and price optimization to the risk the competition, the economy, and more that can affect their customers. Some of the companies that are using this kind of technology are going to include insurers, telecommunications providers, manufacturers, banks, and retailers. When these companies use data mining in the proper manner, it is going to be able to affect each aspect of their business, including customer relationships, operations, revenues, and business models.

How Data Mining Works

So, why is data mining such an important process to focus on? You will see the staggering numbers when it comes to the volume of data that is produced is doubling every two years. Just by looking at unstructured data on its own, but just because we have more of this information does not mean that we have more knowledge all of the time. With the help of data mining, you can do some of the following tasks:

Sift through all of the noise, whether it is repetitive or chaotic, that is found in your data.

You can understand better what is relevant in all of that information, and then make good use of the information to help you assess what outcomes are the most likely for your needs.

It can help you to accelerate the pace of making decisions that are informed and driven by data, and more likely to help your business to thrive and grow.

Now we need to take a look at how this data mining works. We are not able to just grab the data and have these trends shown to us without any additional work. This is where data mining is going to come into play. Data mining is going to involve us exploring and then analyzing a large block of information in the hopes of getting trends and patterns out of that information that is meaningful. We can use the process of data mining in a variety of ways based on what industry the company is in, what they do to serve the customer, and so much more.

For example, data mining can be used to help us discern the opinion, and the sentiment of our users can help with detecting fraud, credit risk management, email filtering with spam, and database marketing to name a few things. All of these are important to many industries and can help them to become more efficient in their jobs while being able to serve the customer even better in the long run.

The process of data mining is going to be broken down into five different steps. In the first step, the company is going to collect the data, and then make sure that it is loaded up properly into their data warehouse. When that is done, they will store and manage the data, either using the cloud or some of the servers they have in-house.

At this point, the IT professionals, management teams, and business analysts are going to access the data and then will determine the best way to organize that information. Then application software is able to come in and sort out the data, based on the results of the user. In the last step, the end-user is going to present the data and all of the findings that were done in the other steps, in a format that is easy to share and usually understand in the form of some kind of visualization like a table or graph.

The next thing that we need to work on is data warehousing and mining software. The programs that you use with data mining will work to analyze the patterns and the relationships that are found in the data, and it is going to do this based on the request of the user. For example, a company may use some of this software in order to create some new classes of information.

To help us illustrate this a bit more, let's imagine that we are a restaurant that would like to use the process of mining data in order to determine the best times to offer specials. The restaurant is going to look at all of the information it has been able to collect based on their specials and how these specials do at different times of the day, and then will create some classes based on when customers visit, and what the customers are going to order when they come to eat.

We can take this a bit further as well. In some cases, a data miner is going to be able to find clusters of information based on a logical relationship, or they may see if there are sequential patterns and associations to draw conclusions about trends in the behavior of the consumer.

Warehousing is going to be another important aspect of data mining. Warehousing is a simple process, and it is basically when a company will centralize their data into one program or one database, rather than having the information spread out between more than one place. With the warehouse for data, an organization may spin off segments of the data for specific users to look over and analyze on a regular basis, and for the specific users to use when they would like.

However, we can also see that the analyst can do another thing during this process as well. For example, sometimes an analyst may start with the data that they would like, and then they can go through and create a data warehouse that is based on those specs. No matter how a business, or even some other entities, organize their data, they use it to support the processes for making decisions with the management of the company.

With this in mind, we also need to take some time to explore examples of data mining along the way. A good example of this is grocery stores. Many of the supermarkets that we visit on a regular basis are going to give off free loyalty cards to customers. These are beneficial to the customers because it provides them with access to prices that are reduced, and other special deals that non-members at that store are not going to be able to get.

But these cards are also going to be beneficial for the store as well; it is going to make it easier for the company to track which customers are buying what, when they are in the store making the purchase, and at what price they are making the purchases for. After receiving all of this data and having a chance to analyze it the stores can then use this kind of data to offer customers coupons targeted to those buying habits, and they decide when to put certain items on sale, or when it is best for the company to sell them at full price.

This is a great way for both parties to win. The customer is going to enjoy that they can potentially save money and so they will sign up for it. The store is going to enjoy that they get a chance to learn more about the customers and set prices at a point that will bring in more people and make them the most money possible.

There are a few concerns that can sometimes come up when we look at data mining and what it is all about. Some people are concerned about data mining because they worry about the company using the information in the wrong manner. It could also be an issue if the company is not getting a good overall sampling of their information, and then make decisions that are wrong the wrong information in the process.

There are a few key takeaways that we can work here to help us get more out of data mining. Data mining is going to be the process of analyzing a large amount of information in order to help us discern the patterns and the trends that are inside. There is likely a lot of information that is going to be present for a business, and they can get that information from a large number of sources. But just having this information is not going to be enough to help the business get the results that they want.

Instead of just collecting the information and letting it sit there, the company actually needs to be able to find what is inside of all that information. There is likely a lot of topics to discuss inside that information, and you can use it to find trends, and make predictions that are driven by data. This makes the decisions better for your company and makes it more likely that you are going to be able actually to see success with it.

Another thing to consider is that data mining is going to be used by corporations for a lot of different things. The way that the company decides to use the information is going to depend on what they need to accomplish, what they gathered the information for, and more. The company can choose to use this information to help them learn more about what the customer is the most interested in and what they want to buy get. It can even come in handy when we talk about spam filtering and fraud detection.

Who uses data mining?

Data mining is going to be at the heart of many efforts for analytics through a variety of disciplines and industries. In fact, almost everyone is able to use this kind of process to help them sort through the abundance of information that they are storing and to ensure they get accurate predictions and patterns shown out of it.

The first industry that can benefit from data mining is going to be communications. This is definitely a market where the competition is tight, but the answers that are needed to stand out from the crowd are going to be found in your data about the consumer. Telecommunication and multimedia companies can use these analytic models to help them make sense of the mountains of data on the customer they have collected, which will help them to predict the behavior of the customer. This may also help in offering campaigns that are highly targeted and more relevant than ever before.

Insurance companies will often work with this data mining as well. With all of that analytic know-how, these insurance companies are going to be able to solve some complex problems when it comes to customer attrition, risk management, compliance, and fraud, to name a few.

Companies have been able to use techniques from data mining to price products in the most effective manner across business lines and to find new ways to offer products that are competitive to customers who already use them.

Next on the list is going to be education. Education can benefit through the process of data mining, and data science as a whole, in many ways. With unified and data-driven views of student progress, it is easier for educators to predict the performance of their students, often before they even get to the classroom, and the teachers can use this information to develop strategies for intervention to keep them on course and doing well.

Data mining comes into play here because it helps the educators to access data on the student, predicts their level of achievement, and can help the educator figure out which students, or even which groups of students are going to need some extra care and attention in the process.

Manufacturing can also benefit when it comes to working with data mining. Aligning supply plans with demand forecasts is going to be essential, as is the early detection of problems, quality assurance, and investment in brand equity along the way. In many cases, with the help of data mining, these manufacturers can predict the wear of production assets and come up with a good schedule of maintenance ahead of time. This helps them to plan ahead and get the work done before a breakdown in the machine happens, maximizing uptime and keeping the production line going and on schedule as much as possible as things go through the day.

We may also see the use of data mining when it comes to banking and the financial world. There are already a number of automated algorithms out there that help banks better understand their base of customers, as well as the billions of transactions at the heart of this whole system. Data mining is able to help with these financial services and the companies that run them by providing a better view of the risks in the market, can help to find fraud faster, manages the obligations the institution has for regulatory compliance, and can ensure that the company gets optimal returns on all of their marketing investments to the customer.

And finally, we can take a look at how data mining is used in retail. Retail companies can take in a lot of information over all of the various customers they work with throughout the year. This results in a large database of the customers, which holds a lot of hidden customer insight that will help you to improve relationships with these customers, optimize the campaigns that you do for marketing, and can even help you to forecast the sales that you can expect in the future.

Through models of data that become more accurate all of the time, these retail companies can offer campaigns that are more targeted. This ensures that they will find that perfect offer that will actually reach the right customer, hopefully at the right time, and will end up making the biggest impact on that particular customer.

All of these industries may be seen as very different, but they do all come together and work to show us just how prominent data mining and data science really are, and why we would want to use these in our own work on a regular basis. It may seem like a lot of work and something that we don't want to waste our time on, and we may wonder if perhaps there are easier and better ways to handle all of the data we want to work with, but when it comes to gathering up some of the useful and relevant pieces of information inside a large set of data,

data mining is one of the best choices to go with.

And the final point that we need to take a look at here is the idea that data mining programs are helpful because they are going to break down the patterns and the connections that are found in the data, and they can get this work done based on the information that the user is going to be able to provide or request at the time.

Chapter 5: Regression Analysis

As you work with a few of the different parts that come with data analysis, you are likely to run into the idea of a regression analysis. This is going to be one of the techniques that you can use with predictive modeling, and it is going to help us look at the relationship that is there between a dependent variable, which is the target, and an independent variable, which is the predictor. This is a big technique that is going to help us with time series modeling, especially with forecasting and the causal effect relationship that will show up with our variables. For example, we may be able to take a look at the relationship that shows up between rash driving and how many accidents happen on the road, and we can study this with regression.

This kind of analysis is going to be a very important tool that we can use for analyzing and modeling the data we want to work with. This analysis though, is meant to help us really see what kind of relationship is going on between at least two variables, but it is possible that more are going to be present. The best way to understand how this all will work together is through the following example.

Let's say that you are looking at a company and you would like to estimate the growth in sales they are having, based on the conditions that are going on right now in the economy. You have the data that is most recent for the company, and this information tells you that the growth in sales is actually about two and a half times the growth that we are currently seeing in the economy.

This is a great thing for the business because it shows how well things are going. We can use this kind of insight in order to make a prediction, assuming that all other things are going to stay constant, on how the future sales of the company will do, based on that past and current information.

There are a lot of benefits that come with using this kind of regression analysis. But the two most common benefits that we will see include:

This analysis is going to indicate to us those significant relationships that happen between both the independent variable and the dependent variable.

This kind of analysis is going to indicate the strength of impact on multiple independent variables on that one dependent variable that is in your problem.

Regression analysis is also going to allow us to compare the effects of variables measured on the different scales, such as the effect of price changes and the number of activities that you do that are promotional. These benefits will make it easier for the data scientist, or the data analyst, or the market researchers to eliminate and then evaluate the best set of variables that can be used for building up our predictive models.

With this in mind, we need to take a look at some of the different techniques that fit under this idea and how they are all used to help a company make some good predictions. These techniques are all going to be driven by three main metrics, including the number of variables you have that are dependent, the type of variable that is dependent, and the shape of the line for your regression. We will discuss these a bit more as we go through this chapter and see what is available at each part. To start, though, we need to take a look at the most common types of regression that you can work with, and how each of them will come into play with your work.

Linear Regression

This is actually one of the most common out of the modeling techniques. Linear regression is actually something that you will hear on a regular basis when it comes to doing some of the predictive modeling. With this technique, we will take the variable that is dependent and see that it is continuous. Then the independent variable, or more than one variable, can either be discrete, or it can also be continuous like the dependent variable. The nature of the regression line will be linear.

The linear regression that we are looking at is responsible for finding the relationship between our dependent variable, and at least one other independent variable, and it is going to use the best fit straight line to make it happen. A good way to visualize this is a graph with a lot of different dots, which will represent your data points. Then there is one line that goes through the middle, trying to match up with as many points as possible.

Of course, this line is not going to be able to hit all of the points of data. You are working with a straight line, and the points of data can be all over the place based on how they fit on the chart. But the idea here is to kind of find the average, and the point where many of the data points as possible are going to match up together and agree. Sometimes this line is slightly curved towards the end to catch a few more points, but it is best to see this one as a straight line, for now, one that is set up to take on as many points as possible.

A few points that we can keep in mind when it comes to the linear regression will include:

We need to see a linear relationship when it comes to our dependent and independent variables.

If you are working with multiple regression, it will suffer from autocorrelation and multicollinearity.

Linear regression is going to be a bad choice sometimes because it will be sensitive to the outliers. This can really affect the regression line, and in the end, if it is not handled in the proper manner, it is going to affect the forecasted values that you get.

This multicollinearity is going to increase how much variance is found in the estimate, and it will make it so that the estimate is sensitive to even small changes that happen in the model. The result of this is that the coefficient estimates that you try to work within this process are not going to be as stable as you may like.

When we are working with more than one independent variable, we can go with the stepwise approach, the backward elimination, and the forward selection to help you to deal with most of the important independent variables.

Logistic Regression

This kind of regression is going to be used to help us find the probability that an event is going to happen or fail. You will use this kind of regression when you have a binary dependent variable. This means that one of the answers is 0 and one is 1. You can choose which of these is true and which one is false, but those are the only two answers that are going to be able to show up in this case.

A few of the things that you can learn about the logistic regression to help make it a bit easier to use, and to see when it is best to work with this one compared to some of the others will include:

This kind of regression is going to be used for a lot of classification problems.

Logistic regression is not going to require us to have a relationship between the independent and dependent variables. It is able to handle the different types of relationships that show up because it is going to come in and apply the non-linear log transformation to the predicted odds ratio.

To make sure that the issues of underfitting or overfitting do not happen, we need to make sure that we include all of the significant variables. A good way to make sure that this happens is to use the stepwise method to estimate our logistic regression.

This kind of regression is going to require us to work with a sample size that is large. This is because the maximum likelihood estimates are not going to be as powerful or as accurate when we use some of the smaller sample sizes.

The independent variables should not be correlated with one another. We do have the option, however, to include interaction effects of categorical variables in our model and in our analysis if this is going to make a difference.

If the dependent variable ends up being multiclass, then it is going to be changed to a Multinomial Logistic regression instead of the logistic regression.

Polynomial Regression

Next on the list is going to be the polynomial regression. This is going to be when the power of the independent variable ends up being higher than 1. In this technique for regression, we will see that the best fit line is not going to be straight like what we talked about in the linear regression. Rather, this one is going to be more of a curve that tries to fit in more of the points of data to get a better result. To help us see more about how this type of regression is meant to work, let's look at a few key points:

While it is tempting to come in and fit a higher degree polynomial to get a lower rate of error, this is going to give us the result of overfitting in the process. Always plot the relationship to see the fit and then focus on making sure that the curve fits the nature of the problem.

It is a good idea to look out for the curve that happens towards the ends and then see whether these shapes and these trends make sense. Sometimes the higher polynomials are going to produce some weird results when you do the extrapolation.

Stepwise Regression

This is a type of regression that is going to be used at any time that we would like to deal with a lot of independent variables at the same time. In this kind of technique, the selection of these independent variables is going to be done using the automation process, which is going to involve us using no kind of human intervention in the process.

This feat may seem like a tall order, but it is achieved by the data scientist by observing some of the statistical values like AIC metrics, t-stats, and R-square to help us discern which variables are the most important. The stepwise regression is basically responsible for fitting the regression model by either dropping or adding in the co-variates one at a time, based on the criteria that you set up ahead of time. Some of the methods that fit under the term of stepwise regression that is the most commonly used will include:

Standard stepwise regression. This one is responsible for helping us do two things. It is going to help us to either remove or to add in predictors as is needed during all of the steps.

Forward selection. This one is going to take the predictor that is the most significant to start, and then will add in variables for each step as needed in the model.

Backward elimination. This one is going to start with all of the predictors already being found in the model and then will start taking some out. It will start out with the least significant variable during each step until you decide it is done.

The aim of working with this kind of technique for modeling is to maximize the prediction power with the minimum number of predictor variables. This one is a good one to choose when you want a method capable of handling higher dimensionality of the set of data.

Lasso Regression

This one is similar to some of the other regressions that you can work with, and it is also able to penalize the absolute size of the regression coefficients. In addition to doing this task, it is going to be able to reduce how much variability is found in your work and can improve the amount of accuracy that we can see with the models that rely on linear regression like what we talked about earlier.

The Lasso regression is going to be a bit different than the ridge regression, if you have worked with this one before, because it is going to use absolute values in the penalty function, rather than relying on the squares all of the time. This leads to penalizing or constraining the sum of the absolute values of the estimates, values that cause some of the parameter estimates to turn out as exactly zero.

The larger the penalty that we find, the further the estimates are going to be shrunk down before they get to absolute zero. This is going to result in variable selection out of given variables for this time. In addition to sharing this kind of information about the Lasso regression, we can also remember a few other key points about it, including the following:

The assumption of this kind of regression is going to be the same as least squared regression, but the normality is not something that we are going to assume.

This regression type is going to take your coefficients and then shrink them down to zero, which is going to make it easier when it is time to select some of the features.

This is a method of regularization, and you will see that it uses these kinds of formulas as well.

If you have a group of predictors that ends up being correlated really well, then the lass model is going to come into play and only pick out one of them to help make things happen. Any of the others that are there will be taken and shrink it down to zero.

As you can see here, there is a lot that you can consider when it comes to working with regressions and how they will be able to take the data that you have accumulated for a long period of time, and ensure that you can gain some powerful insights out of it. You have to choose which of the regression analysis you would like to work with, based on the type of data that you want to focus on, and what information you are trying to gather out of that set of data as well. Take a look at some of the regression formulas and information that we discussed above to help you really see what is available with this kind of analysis over your data.

Chapter 6: Why Is Data Visualization So Important When It Comes To Understanding Your Data?

Now that we have a good idea of what data science is all about, and some of the different steps that need to be taken in order to find the data you want, search through it and come up with the insights that are found inside, it is time to understand the importance, and why we would want to use, data visualization in this process as well. Data visualization is going to be the presentation of data in a format that is either graphical or pictorial. Using this is going to enable those who make the decisions to see all of the analytics from the data presented in a visual manner.

While anyone could go through and read the information on the data and see what is inside on their own, often it is much easier to go through and actually see the information that is there is a visual form. With visualization that is interactive, it is easier to take the concept a bit further using technology to drill down into the graphs and charts to get more details in the process interactively changing up the data you see and the way it is processed to see what that means for the company.

Data visualization is going to be so important simply because of the way that the brain is able to process information. Using graphs and charts to help us visualize large amounts of data is easier compared to pouring over reports and spreadsheets all of the time. This process is a quick and easy way for us to convey concepts in a universal manner. You can often make small changes to the visuals to see what would happen in different situations as you move along. This makes it easier to compare several decisions to pick out the one that is best for your company.

In addition to making it easier for us to understand what is going on with the data, data visualization can help out with a few other tasks as well. Some of the tasks that data visualization is especially good at helping out with will include:

Identifying areas that need improvement or more attention.

Clarifying which factors are the most likely to influence the behaviors of the customer.

Helping you to understand which products should be placed in different locations throughout the store.

Making it easier to come up with predictions when it comes to sales volume.

There are already a lot of different ways that this data visualization is being used. Regardless of the size of the industry, or even what industry you are in, businesses can take data visualization and use it. Any time that you want to go through a large amount of data and figure out what is inside of it, using the other processes that we have already talked about in this guidebook, it is often a good idea to use data visualization along with it as well. This makes it much easier to understand what information is inside of the data and can help you to see better results in no time.

The first way that this data visualization is being used is to help us comprehend the right information quickly. By using a graphical representation of the information your business has, you can get a clear view of a large amount of data. The information is more cohesive, and it is written out or shown in a way that our brains can understand better than a long list or spreadsheet of numbers and data. We can then look at these visuals and draw accurate conclusions based on what we see.

All data scientists and business owners will agree that it is much easier and much faster to analyze information that comes in some kind of visual format - such as a graph - than it is to look at this same information when it is in a spreadsheet or listed out for you to look over. Because of this fact, these visuals are going to make it easier for a business to address any problems that come up or answer the important questions in a timelier manner as well.

The next benefit that comes with using these visuals is that they are there to identify relationships and patterns, in an easy to read format, out of all the data you have collected. Even when we are using a very large and extensive set of data, we can start to make more sense out of it when it has been presented to us in a graphical manner. Businesses become better at recognizing what is there, seeing the relationships that show up, and even seeing which parameters are highly correlated.

Of course, sometimes the correlations are going to be easy to see, and we would be able to catch them in another format as well. But sometimes the correlations are harder to see, and we may miss out on them, and the important insights that we need, if we didn't first put the insights and data into a visual form. Identifying these kinds of relationships will make it easier for an organization to focus on areas that are the most likely to influence their other important goals as well.

The third benefit of using these visualizations and seeing how they are used is that, when a data scientist goes through the information properly and uses the right kind of visual, they are going to help us see the emerging trends early on. Using data visualization to help us discover trends, both in the market and in our own business, is going to really help to beat out the competition, especially if you are one of the first to see these trends before any of your competitors can jump on board.

When you can beat out the competition, simply by seeing the trends in the data you are already collecting, this is one of the best ways to improve your bottom line. With these visualizations, you will easily be able to see some of the outliers on the charts, especially the ones that will affect product quality or customer churn. From there, you can easily find ways to address these issues before they become really big problems that you have to handle and can ensure that you will be able to find new products and services that actually meet where your customers are.

And the fourth way that this is being used is to help communicate a story to others. Once a business has had a chance to take all of their data and uncovered some of the insights that are in there through visual analytics, the next step that we need to take a look at is the best way to communicate all of those trends and insights to other people. Using graphs, charts, and other visual representations that will make an impact and can showcase the data is going to be really important because it's more engaging, helps others to get the message easier, and can help make sure that everyone who sees the information is on board with the new plan.

With this in mind, we now need to go through and lay out the groundwork that is needed for data visualization. Before you try to implement any technology that is new, there are a few steps that we need to go through and take to make sure it all works out. For example, it is not enough to have a solid grasp of the data in front of you, and it is also important to have a good understanding of your goals, audience, and needs.

Taking the time to prepare your organization for this kind of technology to make these visualizations is not always as easy as you might like. Before you can implement it, there are a few things that you need to do first, including the following:

You need to have a good understanding of the data that you would like to visualize. This is going to include the size of the data you want to work with, and the cardinality or the uniqueness of the values of data in a column that you would like to use.

You need to be able to determine what you would like to visualize during this process, and what is the information type that you want to communicate in the charts and graphs and other visualizations that you would like to you.

You need to take some time to know your audience and then understand how these individuals are going to process their visual information. If you are showing this information to a group of data scientists, you may not need the visualization as much because they would know the tables of data and be fine. But if you are showing to the shareholders or to customers, or others who are not professionals in the data science world, then having more of these visualizations can be important.

You need to make sure that your vision is going to convey the information that you want to share in the best and the simplest form to your chosen audience.

Once you have been able to answer these initial questions about the data type that you have, and the audience whom you plan to show this information to, you then need to take some time to prepare for the amount of data that you would like to work with as well. Remember, many times a company is going to have their hands on a large amount of data, thanks to the ease of collecting this data in our modern world, and the inexpensive data storage that is available to them. This means that when you are working on creating your own data visualization, you are likely to have a ton of data that you need to sort through and use ahead of time.

Big data is great because it brings in more insights to the company and can help them to really see what their customers want at that time, but it does bring in some new challenges to the visualization that you are trying to do. This is because large volumes, different varieties, and varying velocities must be considered with this. Plus, it is common that the data is going to be generated at a pace that is much faster than what we can do while managing and analyzing it as well.

There are other factors that you need to consider as you go through this process, such as the cardinality of the columns that you want to add in and try to visualize. High cardinality is going to mean that in your data, there is already a large percentage of values that are unique. This could include something like bank account numbers because each of the account numbers is going to be a unique item. Low cardinality is going to be on the other side of things, and this means that there is going to be a large percentage of repeat values, such as in the column that would list out genders, either male or female, because those are the only two options.

While we are on this topic, we need to take a look at some of the most popular types of visualizations that you can use in data science. All of these can be great for helping you to sort through your data and see what it really means, in a visual form rather than with lots of words and numbers. The method that you choose to go with and the visualization that you decide to pull out is going to depend on your data and what you hope to learn from it. Some of the most common types of visualizations that you can use to understand better the data you have will include:

The scatterplot. This type of visualization is going to be used to help us find the relationship in bivariate data. It is often a good one to use to help us see correlations between two continuous variables.

Histogram: This one is going to show us the distribution that is there with a continuous variable. You can use this one to help you discover the frequency distribution that is there for one single variable when you are in an analysis that is univariate.

Bar chart: This can be called a bar plot or a bar chart. It is going to be used in order to represent data that is categorical with either horizontal or vertical bars. It is going to be a general plot that is going to help you aggregate the data that is categorically based on some function and the default that is going to be the mean.

Pie chart. You can use the pie chart to help represent the proportion of each category when it comes to data that is categorical. You are going to see this as a circle that is divided into slices based on the different parts so you can see how they will be in relation to one another.

Count plot: With the count plot, we are going to see something that is similar to what is possible with the bar plot, except that we only pass the X-axis and the Y-axis represents explicitly counting the number of occurrences. Each bar is going to represent the count for each category of species.

Boxplot: Next on the list is going to be the boxplot. This one is a good visualization to work with when it comes to seeing how the distribution of your variable is going to look. This is kind of a standardized way that we can display the distribution of data based on the five-number summary. This summary will show the maximum, the third quartile, the median, the first quartile, and the minimum.

These are the top types of visualizations that you can work with to help sort through and better understand the information that is hidden in your data. It is possible that you will be able to find other visualizations that work better for the data that you are trying to present, and it is just fine to work with these as well to help you see some better results. You have to choose the visualization option or method that works best for your needs.

Learning about these different options with visualization is so important it will help you to learn when is the best time to use each of these visualizations for data science, and will make it easier for you to really decide which one is the best based on what information you would like to show, and what data you are looking for.

Now all data is going to lend itself to the pie chart very well, for example. If you want to see how prices have gone up in the past ten years, then the pie chart would not be the best, but a line graph or a scatter plot may be the best option that you want to work with. But if you want to see how several parts can come together and how they will relate to one another, then you want to work with some of these visuals to help you understand what is going on, and to see the relationship right away, rather than having to try and read through all of the numbers to make it happen.

Visuals are going to be one of the best things that you can do when it comes to finishing up your work with data science. This is one of the best ways for you to take the information that you gathered, and the analysis that you did, and put it in a form that everyone, whether they are a data scientist or not, is going to be able to understand what you found out. When business leaders and owners want to see what work a data scientist did, and they are interested in seeing what options they should consider with their business and growth in the future, then these visualizations are going to be the best option to make this happen. Picking the right kind of visualization and knowing what it is going to be able to show out of your information, can make a big difference in how well you can show and explain your results.

Chapter 7: Data Science Operations

In this chapter, our discussion will primarily emphasize on building an understanding of the working of the data science process by comprehensively reviewing the steps of the data science process. In other words, the main goal of this chapter will be to outline a comprehensive yet not too technical overview of the data science process without taking the big data context into account. After understanding the data science process properly, we will learn how to work with the most common categories of data, such as big datasets, streaming data, and text data in the upcoming chapters.

Overview of the Data Science Operations

The first and foremost priority when working on a data science project is to take a structured approach and properly follow it as it not only maximizes the project's chances of success, but the cost at which the project is built is also relatively low. Moreover, a structured approach opens up room to bring in teamwork as each team member can be assigned a task on which they are good at. However, this does not mean that the structured approach is a holy grail and is good for every data science project. There may be cases where there are better options than the structured approach, but it is viable for the majority of the data science projects.

The classic data science process has three major steps which we already discussed quite briefly in the first chapter, and these are:

1.   Setting the research goal
2.   Retrieving data
3.   Data preparation
4.   Data exploration
5.   Data modeling
6.   Presentation and automation

We will now briefly introduce each main step and discuss them in detail afterward.

1. The first and foremost plan of action for a data science project is to establish a clear research goal so that all the stakeholders can get the answers to what, how, and why's regarding the project. This step is especially given due importance to significant and big data science projects.

2. After defining the goal of the research, the next thing to do is gather the data resources for analysis. For this purpose, the team handling the project will need to consider suitable data sources that are accessible.

3. However, the collected data is still unrefined and raw. Hence it needs to be filtered and polished before it can be used for analysis, and this is the third step in the data science process, i.e., preparing the data. In this step, we take the raw data and convert it accordingly so that it is usable in our model. While preparing the data, we come across many discrepancies and errors, and all of them need to be sorted out before we

can use it. Moreover, we will also need to incorporate different data sources into the raw data to improve its quality in the case where the collected data is limited or low quality.

4.   After preparing the data for use, the next step is to build a comprehensive understanding of this data sample, in other words, exploring the many aspects of the sample. Exploration of data in this context basically means to qualitatively go through the data and looking for the patterns, correlations, and deviations present within it. These elements can be figured out by using visual and descriptive techniques. After gaining a useful insight into the data, we can use it on our models more effectively.

5.   This is the step where you put all the knowledge you gained from the previous step to good use and begin data modeling, or in other words, building a model based on this data to make predictions according to the charter of your project.

6. The final step is to gather the results procured from the model and present it to the audience. Moreover, to get better results or improve the existing results, one may need to perform the project multiple times. Hence, instead of performing every iteration manually, we can just automate it.

These six steps of the data science process hold up for the ideal scenario. In the real world, the situation might be different as the data scientist following this process might not be able to follow these steps linearly and chronologically by going back and forth the different steps of the process.

The Steps of the Data Science Process

The First Step: Preparing Research Goals and Creating the Project

In this section, we will discuss the previously mentioned steps of the data science process and discuss them in detail. The very first step of the process emphasizes the very essence of the data science project by asking three questions, i.e., what expectations does the company have from your project? Why should the company's management even consider supporting your project? Is this project a subsidiary of another bigger project, or is it a concept pushed by a single person? These questions are basically the crux of what the first step of the data science process is all about.

By clarifying these questions to the audience or respective members of the organization, everyone arrives at the same page of discussion, and the decision to choose the best course action for this project becomes easy to make. Moreover, by obtaining a comprehensive understanding of the project's contextual realms such as a timetable describing the plan of action of the entire project, which is then placed into a charter.

Understanding the Research Goals and Context

One of the most important and essential goals expected from the first step of the data science process is to ultimately create an understanding of the actual grounds on which the project has been created and describe its purpose in an evident and direct fashion (in a document or charter). The most successful way to approach this step is to continue asking yourself questions regarding the project and researching the answers, in this way, you can develop a better understanding with a more in-depth analysis of every aspect. Furthermore, one should not take this phase of the project for granted even in the slightest manner as you will be spending a lot of time researching the questions asked in the initial business meeting or group meeting and when you finally come up with a brilliant answer, it would all be wasted if you later come to know that you had misinterpreted the original queries put forth by the others. This phase has the highest percentage of failure for data scientists as compared to the other steps in the data science process. This is due to the fact that despite data scientists being brilliant and mathematically intelligent, they often fail to comprehend the context of business goals.

Creating a Project Charter

Sponsors and clients often prefer to be given a direct and to the point description of what they are supporting and putting out funds for. As such, once the business agreement has been established and accepted, it is important to be direct with them in matters such as a formal agreement on the deliverables. The most effective way to address this situation is to use a project charter that houses all the important information with regards to the project, and this is always practiced for data science projects of significant importance and magnitude.

Creating a project charter is not something that can be done by a single person, in fact, it is a team effort, and the contribution of each team member ultimately results to a charter that emphasizes the following aspects:

1.   An intelligible research goal

2.   The project's purpose and its context

3.   The method through which the data scientists will carry out the analysis

4.   The resources which will be consumed are outlined

5.   Evidence backing that the project is do-able and can be performed or giving conceptual proof for the project

6.   Deliverables and the chances of its success

7.   A detailed timeline of the project

This information will enable the client or sponsor to work out the necessary funds required for this project, along with the manpower and data resources required to make this project a success.

Step 2: Retrieving the Data

After the project is approved and the research goals have been thoroughly researched, the next thing to do is securing a source of data for the project. Often times, data scientists will be able to procure a data source, or the company they are working for will already have arranged a data source for them easily collect and store the required data. However, there might be rare cases where the data scientist himself will have to create a data collection process out in the field. Moreover, the data scientist doesn't need to be bound to use the data collected by his organization only if he feels that something's missing or the data source is insufficient. He can always look towards third parties and other organizations and, if need be, buy the data.

In this step, you are mainly concerned with just acquiring the data; it can be either in the form of a document or a well-designed table.

Check the Data Stored Within the Company

The company in which the data scientist is employed should be the very first place to look for data. Most of the time, companies sort out, clean, and store data in an orderly fashion for later use, and this data is easy to collect and use in data science projects. Companies usually store their data in official repositories (databases, data marts, data warehouses, and data lakes) of data and are often maintained by a group of IT professionals. While the primary function of different data repositories is the same, i.e., data storage, they differ in other aspects. For instance, a database is mainly used to only store data while a data warehouse is used to store and analyze data at the same time. Similarly, data marts are a subsidiary of data warehouses and are used by specific business units. Moreover, data warehouses and data marts are used to store data that is preprocessed, and data lakes store data in its original, unprocessed, raw format.

Although companies can readily give access to the necessary data required for the data science project, finding, and retrieving the data can still be difficult in some cases. For instance, a company that is growing will often have its data scattered in different places, and employees always keep changing; hence the knowledge of the stored data is also dispersed. Hence, a data scientist will have to do some investigation and find out about the lost or missing pieces of data and collect them. One other option, in this case, would be to retrieve data from third parties or other organizations and incorporate that data into the original data source to improve its quality or complete it.

One more tough issue faced by data scientists are being given restricted access to data. Organizations emphasize the importance and sensitivity of data and, accordingly, follow policies so that each person only gets as much access to the data as he needs. Such policies are termed as 'Chinese walls' and can be either in the form of physical or digital barriers. These protective measures are not a bad thing, however, for a data scientist, they become an obstacle, and it might take time to get proper authorization to access the complete data source.

Checking Elsewhere for Data

It's not always the case that the data to be used for the project should only be from the company's database. Most of the time, the company does not have a data source that can be used in the project, and in such cases, consulting organizations that specialize in data collection is the most optimal choice. However, not every company sells data for money; some companies might even give out high-quality data for free. All you need to do is look in the right places.

Similarly, some companies value data as an asset that is more valuable than fuel. However, companies and governments still hand out data for free by sharing their databases. However, the quality depends on company to company. This data is very useful for improving the quality of the original data. In addition, if someone wants to work on and improve their data science skills locally, then they can also use this data as practice.

Below is a table that lists a few of the open-data providing companies. For beginner data scientists, collecting data from these sources will serve as a very useful experience.

Performing Data Quality Checks

In most cases, the data scientist will spend about 80% of his time in correcting the errors in his data, cleansing and refining it. Although this is a step that is to be performed formally in the 3rd stage of the process, it is always a good idea to do some quality checks of the data while it is still being retrieved to avoid problems in the future. As this is a time-consuming step, doing pre-emptive data error correction and cleansing can save a lot of time in the following steps, and you can focus on more intricate discrepancies in the data in the actual data refining phase of the process. Furthermore, the majority of the errors that you'll see in the data are easy to identify, but if you become careless in this step, a lot of your time will be consumed in fixing these easy to spot errors that could have been prevented in the data import step.

The difference between this pre-emptive data investigation and the actual data exploration in the next phase lies in the goal and depth of the data investigation being done. In this pre-emptive investigation, our goal is to check if the data being imported matches the data source and see if the data we are retrieving is in the correct format. Once we have procured enough evidence that tells us of the imported data's similarity to the data source, then we stop checking. In the actual data preparation phase, our goal is to explore the data in more detail and do a detailed error correction check. If we properly performed the pre-emptive error checking, then the discrepancies found in the data in this phase indicate that these errors are also found in the source document itself. Hence our focus now will be on the content variables and other such data entry errors. Once we have prepared the data, we begin to learn what we can from it in the exploratory phase. Once we have assumed that the data we are studying is clean and free of errors, then we can statistically analyze it by considering elements such as distributions, correlations, and outliers.

Step 3: Cleansing, Integrating and Transforming Data

An accurate phrase to describe the data which was collected in the retrieval phase is "A diamond in the making." This accurately depicts the nature of the data. If we properly care for it, clean it, integrate data from other sources to enrich its quality and transform it accordingly to fit it in our model, the data will become a valuable asset in our project. Hence, in this phase, our major concern is to turn this raw data into something useful and beneficial to our project. In other words, we will be spending our time cleansing and converting this data to be used in the following reporting and modeling phases of the process. Performing this step properly is very crucial as it will not only save our time in the upcoming phase, but the performance of our model also depends on this data, hence the finer quality data we procure, the better our model works. If we put in bad data into the model, then we should only expect useless and bad results in return.

The model can never use the data in its current format when we are preparing or refining it, hence performing data transformation is always necessary so that we can use this data in our model; otherwise, everything we have done up till now will be useless.

In the mind map figure above, multiple actions are detailing how to perform data cleansing, data transformation, and combining data. We will now discuss these actions in detail.

Data Cleansing

Data cleansing is the process where the data is cleansed and refined in order to take out all the junk from it and ensure that the results given by this data are useful to our project. In most cases, there are generally two types of error which are most commonly observed in data.

The first type of error is 'interpretation error.' This error usually lies with the data proof-reader going through the collected data. Such a person generally reads a value and takes it for granted, for instance, reading that the average lifespan of a person is 200 years.

The second type of error is 'inconsistencies.' This error points to the discrepancies between the different data sources being used or to the standardized values being used by the company from where the data has been collected. For instance, a data table showcasing two item groups, 'Female' and 'F.' Both of these values represent the same thing; however, they are still being used in the same data table. Another is that in the data source, one table is using the currency of Pounds while the very next data table is using the currency of Dollars. There are a lot of these errors all around the data, and they need to be fixed.

Here's a table showcasing some of the most common data errors along with their possible solutions.

A data scientist can also use advanced techniques in order to handle these errors, such as 'simple modeling.' Similarly, plotting diagnostic graphs can also give us insight into such errors in the data sample. For instance, consider the following figure showcasing a graph that calculates and identifies the discrepancies in the data points.

To get familiar with the data sample, we perform regression and analyze the resulting regression line in the graph. This regression line carries information regarding the individual impact of the data points on the line itself. When a single data point is observed to have a greater impact on the regression line, this indicates that there is an error within the data, and this data point can guide us to that error. But this data point doesn't need to be always an error; it can also be a valid point. However, using such methods to clean data can be a bit too resource consuming as other simple methods can be used as well. We will now proceed to explain the common data errors in more detail.

• Data Entry Errors

The processes that are most prone to errors are the collection of data and data entry. This is because of human input.

Humans are never perfect; they may lose concentration one second and make an error in that window of a second and not notice it. However, collecting data from machines is also not error-free. A human can make an error because of his incompetence while a machine makes an error due to a hardware failure or other technical issues. For instance, a machine collecting data may make an error due to bugs in the extract, transmission errors, during transforming data, or even in the load phase (ETL).

In datasets that are of relatively small sizes, the values can be manually checked and corrected. The errors in the data during analyzing are not diverse and can be easily sorted and detected by simply tabulating the data by using counts. If we are working with data that can have only one of the two states, i.e., either useful or useless, good, or bad, then the frequency table will be able to handle this data most optimally. In the table shown below, we can see a frequency table, and the values 'Godo' and 'Bade' represent the discrepancies in the table.

We can remedy such types of errors by simply using a few lines of if-then-else codes as shown below

```
if x == "Godo":
    x = "Good"
if x == "Bade":
    x = "Bad"
```

• Redundant Whitespaces

One of the most difficult to detect errors to detect are whitespaces, and the most common errors caused by them are redundant characters. These can cause delays that stretch up to multiple delays, and when you finally find the bug in the code, a lot of important time has been used up, which makes it even more difficult to explain it to the stakeholders. This is mainly because the cleansing process during the ETL phase was not done properly, and one of the tables coincidently contained whitespaces leading it to be overlooked. One small slip-up now becomes a time-consuming error. Fixing whitespaces is a relatively easy job in most of the programming languages, but only if they are detected in the early stages of the process. When the code becomes bigger and lengthier, the whitespaces create bigger complications. Programming languages support string functions that specifically eliminate the whitespaces that may be trailing or leading in the strings. In Python, by using the function strip(), we can easily remove these trailing and leading spaces in the strings.

- Capital Letter Mismatches

Another common problem observed is mismatching capital letters. Programming languages are case sensitive, meaning that they do not consider 'America' and 'america' as the same thing. We can easily fix this by using the .lower() function which results in the string coming back in lowercase in Python, for instance

"America".lower() == "america".lower() will result in true.

• Impossible Values and Sanity Checks

Sanity checks are a very important type of data check. This means that you check the data for values that are physically or theoretically not feasible. In other words, we go through the data fixing values that are just not possible, for instance, a person with an age of 230 years or someone who has a height of 5 meters.

Sanity checks are conveniently expressed by rules such as

check = 0 <= age <= 120

• Outliers

Outliers are basically observations that are not following the same pattern as the other relating observations. In other words, these observations are following an entirely different logic than the other observations (in some cases, the process through which these observations are being generated can also be different). One of the most convenient and quickest methods to identify outliers in a data sample is to plot the data into a table with values ranging from minimum to maximum as shown below.

The first bar graph does not show any outliers in the data, but the second bar graph shows the potential outliers on the upper areas of the data where the distribution is expected to be normal. In natural sciences, the most common type of distribution is this normal distribution (also known as Gaussian distribution). Outliers have a significant impact on the data modeling process, and thus, this problem must be sorted out with the utmost priority.

- Handling Missing Values

The missing values in a data sample do not necessarily indicate that the data is incorrect. However, they must not be ignored. While some modeling techniques can handle missing values, others cannot. Missing values point to the fact that there might be a discrepancy in the data retrieval process or during the ETL process. Some of the most common ways data scientists deal with this problem outlined in the table shown below

Technique	Advantage	Disadvantage
Omit the values	Easy to perform	The information is lost after an observation
Set value to null	Easy to perform	This method is not supported by every modeling or implementation technique as they are incapable of handling empty (null) values
Impute a static value such as 0 or the mean	Easy to perform and most of all, we avoid losing information from the other variables in the observation	

This can instigate the model to produce estimations that are false

Take an estimate or theoretical distribution and impute the value from it

This does not affect the model as much as the other techniques It is relatively difficult to properly execute, and the user has to make data assumptions which can give rise to further errors

Modeling the value

This does not affect the model as much as the other techniques This makes the model too confident, raise the dependence of the values on each other artificially and is difficult to execute as well as error-prone because you will be making data assumptions

The choice of technique is entirely up to the data scientist's preference, but the choices made are normally determined by the stage at which the user is correcting the error varies for special cases. For instance, if the data scientist does not have spare observations to lose, then the technique which omits the observation is definitely not the right technique for this case. Furthermore, if the data scientist observes that the missing value can be described on the basis of a stable dimension, then he can impute the missing value on this assumption. In the case of scales, the missing value might be a zero; for instance, a customer has no promotion applied on his shopping cart, so this missing promo value might be a zero, i.e., no price cuts have been applied.

• Deviations from a Codebook

A codebook can be defined as a form of metadata, or put simply, a description of the data. A typical codebook has information relating to the,

• The number of variables present in the data per observation

- The total number of observations in the data

- The meaning of each encoding within a variable (For example, a variable encoded with the value '0' means 'negative' and '5' means 'highly positive')

In large datasets with a codebook or standardized values, recurring errors can be easily identified and dealt with by using a simple set of operations. Moreover, codebooks also give other useful information, such as the type of data we are dealing with.

In cases where a data scientist is dealing with the check and balance of multiple values, then one optimal approach to handle such type of data is to plot the values from the codebook into a table and then use a 'difference' operator on it. In this way, we will be able to easily identify any errors and discrepancies in the values as they will be clearly visible in the tables. Hence, we are harnessing the functionality of tables to our advantage effectively and efficiently.

- Different Units of Measurement

It is important to standardize the units of measurements being used in the data. If the sample we are using for the project has multiple data sources, then there's a high chance that the values might have different units of measurements. For instance, if we are dealing with a data sample that contains information on gasoline prices and the data has been collected from multiple sources. There's a possibility that some of the gasoline price values will be in gallons, and some of the price values will be in liters. Fixing this discrepancy is relatively easy; all you have to do is take a standard value and perform unit conversions on the varying units of measurement.

- Different Levels of Aggregation

This type of error is similar to the different units of measurement discrepancy we discussed previously. To understand this data error more comprehensively, lets briefly put forth an example. Consider that you are working with two separate datasets. In one of these sets, the data is entered as data per week, and in the other set, the data is entered as data per workweek. These two are very different levels of aggregation.

To fix this type of error, we can choose either of the two approaches, i.e., summarizing or expanding.

Data Combining

Usually, the data you find in organizations or any third party is actually collected from multiple different sources, surveys, and other such references. In other words, high-quality data is never obtained from a single source. Hence, if we collect data with mediocre quality and are insufficient for our project, then we can simply incorporate data from other sources into it to improve its quality. In this step, we will be discussing in detail how we can take multiple data sources and integrate them into our sample data. However, bear in mind that combining data from different sources is not as simple as it may sound because the data we are collecting can be in different formats, sizes, shapes, and structures. To integrate it properly, we will have to employ some suitable techniques to standardize them.

For the sake of brevity, we will be only discussing table data as they are not only comprehensive but also the most common type of data structure that you will come across when going through multiple sources. However, this does not mean that we should shrug off the data sources that do not incorporate tables, but for beginners, table data is more than sufficient.

Multiple Ways of Data Combining

To combine data, there are two most common methods used, these methods are operations that are performed on two distinct datasets to conjoin them, and they are:

1.   Joining: as the name suggests, this operation conjoins the information of

two tables together, i.e., the information of one table is incorporated into the data of the other table.

2. Appending or Stacking: this operation stacks or appends the information of a table to the data of the other table. This is not to be confused with the joining operation as it simply merges data together while appending adds the observations of a table to some other table.

• Joining Tables

In joining tables, we enrich the observations of our table by bringing in foreign data sources (tables) and using their observations and combine it with ours. The main focus of this operation is improving the quality of only one observation. Let's discuss this with an example. Consider that you are working with a data sample that's in the form of a table, and this table contains information pertaining to the purchase history of a customer. Now, you are also provided with a table that has data about the customer's residential address. By using the joining operation on these two tables, we can combine the data together, enriching the original data sample so that it can be used in our model.

In order to combine the two tables, we start to identify the common elements and use a single variable to represent these common values, for instance, common names, dates, countries, etc. A term used to describe these common elements is 'key,' and these elements are known as keys. Moreover, if these keys are a unique identifier for some records in the table, then they are termed as 'primary keys.' As we previously discussed in the example, a table can house information such as the purchasing patterns of the customer while the other table contains the demographic data of the customer, and each of these two tables has primary keys that uniquely identify their respective data.

Users that are adept at Microsoft Excel can easily identify such similarities by using the lookup function. Since we are joining two tables together, the resulting size of the table will not remain the same; as such, we can control the output table's shape (the rows or columns) by using specific join types. These join types will be explained in the upcoming sections of the book.

- Appending Tables

The meaning of appending or stacking tables is to essentially take the observations of one table and incorporate them into another table. This is different from combining the tables because we are taking only the data that is relevant to the data in the table, which we are trying to refine. The figure shown below is a common example of appending or stacking tables.

In the example shown above, we can see that the first table contains data of the two client's purchasing history from the month of January only. While the second table also has the same two client's purchasing history data but from the month of February. The second table is added to the first table, and in this way, we append the second table's data to enrich the quality of the first table. To perform appending, we can use the union operation, which is a command used in SQL. Other operations can also perform this task, such as difference and intersection.

•	Using Views to Simulate Joining and Appending

In joining and appending, we are basically duplicating the data of the other table to combine and append it to the first table. In this example, this does not pose an issue, but if a data scientist is working with a table that contains gigabytes or even terabytes of data, then it becomes a very prominent data storage issue. For this very reason, the concept of view was introduced. Views is a tool that allows us to combine the data in the two tables without duplicating it as the process is performed on a virtual layer. In this way, we are avoiding data duplication, and hence, there are no storage complications to deal with. In the figure shown below, you can see that instead of duplicating the sales data from different months, they are being combined into yearly sales data virtually.

However, Views is not a holy grail tool, meaning that it does come with some drawbacks even if it provides such functionality, and that is the tool draws in more processing resources as the tools perform the joining function every time the table is queried while the joining operator performs this function only once.

• Enriching Aggregated Measures

To increase the quality of the data, we can add calculated values to the data, which will not only enrich it but also increase its depth of detail. For instance, calculating the percentage of the total stocks sold in a particular region, etc. and adding it to the table. Going for aggregated measures can exponentially broaden the perspective of the data, which will increase the performance of the data model. The figure shown below details a data set that has been aggregated.

This aggregated data set can be used to determine each product's participation within their respective categories. In this way, we can explore the data in a more definitive manner and also build a better data model. In most of the cases, the data models that are using relative measures (this means percentage calculations) exceed the models that are using raw numbers in terms of performance alone.

Transforming Data

Some data models can only work with data that is in a specific shape, and it is not always necessary that the data will be in the desired shape to begin with.

Hence, we need to transform the data to make it usable in our data modeling process.

Most of the time, to suitably transform our data, we will need to address the estimation problem first and foremost, and the most effective way to do so is by transforming the input variables. However, the relation between the input and output variables is not always simply linear. For example, consider two variables, y and ab^dc (exponential power) in y = ab^dc. This relationship between the two variables is not linear and the best way to deal with the estimation problem in variables with a non-linear relationship, we simply take the log of the independent variables as shown below.

In this way, say that we have two variables x and y with a non-linear relationship, by converting the variable x to log x, the relationship between x and y becomes linear.

Reducing the Number of Variables

There are cases where a model is overloaded with too many variables, and one should know that a greater number of variables do not mean a greater amount of information. A model could have a large number of variables, but the information retained by it would still be less. Moreover, a model becomes unpredictable when there are too many variables, and even some techniques start performing poorly because of this. For example, every Euclidean distance-based technique starts performing poorly after the variable count exceeds 10. In such cases, we need to eliminate some of the variables to reduce the total variable count.

The main focus of the data scientist is to throw out as many variables as possible while maintaining the maximum amount of data within the model. Techniques to do so will be discussed in the next chapter. From looking at the figure shown below, we can see the impact of reducing variables to understand the key values even better.

Moreover, we can see that only two variables are responsible for about 50.6% of the total variation in the dataset, and these two variables are Component1 and Component2. To be more specific, both of these variables are actually combinations of the native variables in the data sample. These variables are also known as 'principal components.'

Transforming Variables into Dummy Variables

The distinctive feature of dummy variables is that they are assigned only one of the two binary values, i.e., either True (1) or False (0). The reason why dummy variables are considered as an option in data transformation is that they can provide us with useful insight into understanding some of the observations easily. In other words, dummy variables are basically used to straight-away identify the categorical absences of classes in a table. This means that a class category can be immediately be identified if it is present or absent in a data table without actually having to go through the data completely. To use dummy variables, we simply create a column inside the existing data table and put the corresponding dummy variables. For example, we have a data table that describes the weekdays on which the observations were made, and all the days are assigned in this table. Now, besides the weekday classes, we will put respective dummy variables to show whether the observation was made on a Sunday or any other day of the week. By putting the True (1) value inside the dummy variable column and False (0) in the other respective columns, we can quickly tell whether the observation was made on this day or not. This technique is commonly used in data modeling and is especially popular with economists.

Below is an example showing the use of dummy variables in a data table.

Step 4: Exploring the Data and Analyzing it

By now, we have properly sorted and refined the data to be used in the project. Now, we have to gain an understanding of what this data actually means to be able to use it more effectively in data modeling. In this step, we will intricately explore the realms of this data and carefully analyze it. Most of the time, data scientists use graphical techniques to study the data as visual stimulation is much easier than just blandly going through numbers and more numbers. In addition, studying the data by using pictorial representations makes it easier to notice and understand the relationship between the variables and their respective interactions. Hence, it is very important to keep our senses sharp and alert throughout this step because we will need to use the knowledge gained in this stage later on, and this is very crucial. Moreover, as you are analyzing the data even more critically, you will come across some discrepancies that you might have missed in the previous step. This is normal, in such cases, all you have to do is take a step back and fix them, then resume the data study.

Like we discussed that visualization techniques have the maximum impact when exploring the data. There are several techniques you can use, such as plain line graphs, histograms, or even Sankey and network graphs, although they are a bit complex. It all depends on what technique suits the data sample the best. In some cases, one might want to gain a detailed and thorough insight into the data sample, and to do this, the recommended technique would be to use simple graphs and make composite graphs from them. In other cases, one might want to explore the data in a more relaxed, simple, and fun way, and to do that, and the recommended technique is to use animated graphs.

These are some simple graphs where data has been plotted to give an idea. To gain more insight, we can make a composite graph made up of these three graphs. This is a common practice in data science and is known as 'overlaying.' In the figure below, you can see a Pareto diagram which has been made from several simple graphs.

Another useful technique to explore data is 'brushing and linking.' In this technique, we first combine different graphs and then link them together. In this way, when a change happens in one graph, the other graphs are also influenced accordingly. An example of such a graphing technique is shown in the figure below.

This example represents the average score of answers to the questions in different countries. These graphs clearly show a relationship between the answers. If we highlight several points in the subplot, then we can observe that these selected points are actually corresponding to similar points in the rest of the graphs. In this specific example, the two points that have been selected in the Q28_1 graph is corresponding to the highlighted points in the Q28_2 and Q28_3 graphs.

Apart from these graphs, histograms and boxplots are also very important. A histogram is a type of graph that takes a variable and separates it into different individual categories. These different categories are then summed up and represented in the graph. A typical histogram graph looks like this:

On the other hand, a boxplot does not provide information regarding the current number of observations. Instead, it gives insight into the distribution of variables in the data within their respective categories, such as minimum, maximum, and median measures. A typical boxplot is shown below.

Although we have only discussed visual techniques so far, there are also non-visual techniques that data scientists use to study data, for example, tabulation and clustering. Even some modeling techniques are used for exploring the data and analyzing it; some data scientists also use plain data models to perform this step.

Step 5: Building the Model

Now that we have cleaned, prepared, transformed, and studies the data properly, we can start creating a data model accordingly. If we have properly performed the previous data science steps, then building the data model will be very specific and focused as we already know what to do with the data and what outcome we expect from the model. The components of the fifth step of the data science process are shown below.

The techniques used and described in this step are basically from the field of machine learning, data mining, and statistics, so having adequate knowledge about these fields mentioned above is also essential for a data scientist. Right now, we will only briefly discuss these techniques. However, we will go into more detail exploring these techniques in the coming chapters. Although it is not possible to incorporate the full conceptual briefing of these fields in this book, the things we do discuss will help in about 80% of the data science projects.

Similar to the data science process, creating a machine learning data model is also an iterative process. The user has the freedom to choose whatever techniques and methods he wishes to use in his model, and the resulting output is a representation of the machine learning techniques used. However, the process of building models is usually made up of 3 main steps:

1. Choosing the variables to feed it into the model and determining the modeling technique to be used.

2. Executing the Model

3. Performing the Diagnosis of the model and comparing its results with other similar models.

Model and Variable Selection

As we discussed in the previous sections, we need to carefully choose the variables that we want to use in the model in such a way that we get the maximum output from the variable while using the least number of variables. Otherwise, the model will be overloaded, and its performance will be diluted. With regards to selecting the proper variables, this should be clear by now as the necessary variables to be used should have already been highlighted while exploring the data. Now, there are a lot of techniques that are available to be used in data modeling and selecting a technique for the project is entirely up to the data scientist's intuition. There are several factors to take into consideration while selecting the proper model for the project and some of these factors are:

• Expected performance

• The project's requirement aligning with the data model

• Choosing the right product environment and considering the ease of implementation

• The maintenance of the model and the grace period through which leaving the model untouched will have no impact

• Whether there is a need for the model to be easily understood by others or not

Once we have considered all these factors, we are now going to proceed to build the model accordingly.

Model Execution

After selecting the type of model we want to build, we will need to execute it in Python code. However, before we can execute the model, we will first need to set up a Python virtual environment and put in the corresponding codes over there. This book assumes that you already know how to set up a virtual environment

Popular programming languages such as Python come pre-loaded with the necessary libraries enabling us to easily execute models. Examples of such libraries are StatsModels and Scikit-learn, and the reason why we use preloaded libraries is that they natively support some of the most successful techniques used in data modeling. For example, if you want to perform linear regression on your own, then you will have to put in a lot of effort, but with the StatsModels and Scikit-learn libraries, all you have to do is implement the following lines of code shown below, and you will easily execute a linear prediction model.

```python
import statsmodels.api as sm
import numpy as np
predictors                              =
np.random.random(1000).reshape(500,2
)
target   =   predictors.dot(np.array([0.4,
0.6])) + np.random.random(500)
lmRegModel = sm.OLS(target,predictors)
result = lmRegModel.fit()
result.summary()
```

This linear regression graphically shown above attempts to fit a line while minimizing the distance to each point.

If we look at this figure a bit closely, then we can see that there is a predictor variable on the horizontal axis and a target variable on the vertical axis, this is because we created and implemented a predictor value that tries to foretell the behavior of the target variables. A little trick that has been used in this example is that the target values themselves have been based on the predictor values, with some randomness being added to the target variables. As a result, we have gotten a model that is well-fitted. To check the outcome of the model, we use the command result.summary() shown as a table below; however, it should also be noted that the result varies depending on the random variable you get in the model.

When you want your model to predict values, then you go with a linear regression model. Similarly, when you want the model's function to be to classify things, then you simply go with a classification model instead. The most popular classification model is the k-nearest neighbor model.

An example of a k-nearest neighbor model is shown below.

K-nearest neighbor models have a bunch of labeled points, and an unlabeled point and the way they work is that the model analyzes all the labeled points nearest to the unlabeled point and then gives a prediction of what the unlabeled point must be.

To create a classifying model, we can do so by using the following lines of code in Python while using the Scikit learn library.

```
from sklearn import neighbors
predictors                          =
np.random.random(1000).reshape(500,2
)
target                              =
np.around(predictors.dot(np.array([0.4,
0.6])) +
  np.random.random(500))
clf                                 =
neighbors.KNeighborsClassifier(n_neighb
ors=10)
knn = clf.fit(predictors,target)
knn.score(predictors, target)
```

In the above lines of code, we created a random predictor data and a somewhat random target data, which is actually based on the aforementioned predictor data and then proceed to fit the model up to 10 nearest neighbors.

The accuracy of the model is 85%, which is really good for our project. To do a more detailed inspection of the model's performance, we can score it by testing it on new data. This can be done by

prediction = knn.predict(predictors)

After getting the prediction, we use a confusion matrix to compare it to the original result.

metrics.confusion_matrix(target,predicti on)

And the output is a 3x3 matrix shown below

Model Diagnostics and Comparison

Usually, when working on data science projects, you will end up building several data models and compare them with each other based on the project's success criteria and choose the one that performs the best among them. A useful trick that can help you pick out the best performing model is to hold back some data when building these different models, meaning that you leave out part of the data in the sample when building the model. After the models have been built, you use this remaining data and test the model on it. So, all of the models will be tested on this unseen data, and corresponding error measures will be calculated to evaluate the model. You can easily get the results showing which one performs best. There are several error measures that can be used, and in the example shown below, the error measure being used is the 'mean square error.'

Mean square error works by analyzing the accuracy of every prediction and squaring the calculated error, then adding up the errors of every one of the predictions.

In the figure shown below, we can see that there are two data models being compared for their performance on predicting the order size from the known data of the price. The sizes of the two models also differ, while the first model's size is 3*price (size = 3*price), the size of the second model is 10 (size = 10). The original data sample consists of a total of 1,000 observations, and out of this data sample, only 80% (or 800) of the observations have been used to train the model, while the rest 200 observations have been used to test the model. The two models are tested after training, and the one with the lowest error is the best suited for the job.

Step No. 6: Presentations of the Findings

This is the part where the hours and months of hard work that you have put into the data science project will finally pay off when you present your findings and results to the stakeholders and audience and be appreciated for your efforts and ingenuity.

There are also times where people appreciate your model and want to see it work again to predict some values, and for this, you will have to perform the data analysis all over again. But since we have already dealt with the initial grunt work, we can now simply automate the model so that it performs the data analysis all on its own. Most of the time, only automating the model scoring will be enough, but you can also create an application that can automatically refresh the model's reports to a proper format such as an Excel spreadsheet, a Word document, or even a PowerPoint presentation. In this stage of the data science process, your software ingenuity will shine the most. It is recommended that you take guidance from books dedicated to polishing these skills as it will greatly help bring your hard work to the audience with full glamour.

Chapter 8: Machine Learning

What is Machine Learning?

Now that we know a bit about data science, it is time to work a bit more with the specifics of machine learning. When it comes to looking at technology, you will find that machine learning is something that is really growing like crazy. You may not have been able to learn much about machine learning in the past, but it is likely that, even if you haven't done much in the world of technology, you have used machine learning in some form or another.

For example, you have probably used this kind of technology when you are using some kind of search engine to look up something online. Machine learning is the best option for you to use to make sure that you are able to make these search engines work for you. The program for the search engine is going to use machine learning to help the user get the search results that they need. And if it is set up in the right way, it is going to learn a bit from the choices of the user, helping it to become more accurate over time.

This is just one of the examples that you are able to see when it comes to technologies that will rely on machine learning. You will find that in addition to working on a search engine, including Google, this technology is going to work with some spam messages and some other applications. Unlike some of the traditional programs that you may have learned how to work within the past, machine learning is going to be able to make adjustments and changes based on the behavior of the user. This helps you to have more options and versatility about the programs that you create.

There are a lot of computers out there that will have machine learning already on them, and you can even program these computers in order to learn from the inputs that the user is going to give it.

The Basics of Machine Learning

Now that we have had some time to go over a few of the basics that come with machine learning, it is time to delve in a bit more and learn how this process works, and why it is so important when you are trying to work on programs that are able to do what you want. When you are working with this kind of programming, you get the benefit of teaching a computer, or even a specific program, how to work with the experiences it has had in the past so that it can perform the way that it should in the future.

A good idea of how to illustrate this in the field is the idea of filtering out spam email. There are a few different methods that a programmer is able to use to make this one work. But one of the best and the simplest versions that you are able to work with for your program is to teach the computer how it is able to categorize, memorize, and then identify all of the different emails that are found in your inbox that you have gone through and labeled as spam. If it is successful, it should, at least most of the time, be able to tell when an email is spam and keep it out of your inbox.

While this is a memorization method that is easy to program, there are still a few things that could fail with it, and make it not work the way that you want. First, you are going to miss out on a bit of inductive reasoning in that program, which is something that must be present for efficient learning. Since you are the programmer, you will find that it is much better to go through and program the computer so that it can learn how to discern the message types that come in and that are spam, rather than trying to get the program to memorize the information.

To make sure that this process of machine learning is easy as possible, your goal would be to program the computer in a way that it is able to scan through any email that comes through the spam folder or any that it has learned is spam over time. From this scan, the program is going to be able to recognize different words and phrases that seem to be common in a message that is spam. The program could then scan through any of the newer emails that you get and have a better chance at matching up which ones should go to your inbox and which ones are spams.

You may find that this method is going to be a bit harder to program and take a bit more time, but it is a much better method to work with. You do need to take the proper precautions ahead of time with it to ensure that when the program gets things wrong (and it will make mistakes on occasion), you are able to go through and fix it fast.

There are many times that a person would be able to take a look at an email and with a glance figure out if it is spam or not. The machine learning program is going to do a pretty good job with this, but it is not perfect. You want to make sure that you are teaching it the right way to look at the emails that you get. And, sometimes, it will send perfectly good emails to the spam folder. But the more practice it gets with this and the more it learns how to work with what is spam and what isn't, the better it is going to get at this whole process.

Are there any benefits that come with machine learning?

There are a lot of different programming options that you are able to work with when it comes to making a program or doing some code. Machine learning is just one of the options that you can work with. With that said, you may be curious as to what are the benefits of working in machine learning rather than one of the other options.

At this point, you are curious as to why machine learning is going to be so great, and why you would want to make sure this is the method that you will use.

There are a lot of options that you can program and code when you are working with machine learning, but we are going to focus on two main ones that are sure to make your programming needs a bit better.

The first concept that we are going to look at is the fact that machine learning means that you are able to handle any kind of task that seems too complex for a programmer to place into the computer. The second one is the idea that you are able to use the things that you learn from machine learning in order to adaptively generate all of the different tasks that you need to do. With these two concepts in mind, let's take a look at some situations where you may want to work with machine learning, where other codes and programming tricks and techniques are just not going to cut it.

Some More Complicated Tasks

The first category that we are going to look at when it comes to using machine learning is with some of the more complicated tasks that come up. There are going to be a few tasks that you are able to work on with your programming skills that, no matter how hard you try, just seem to not mesh together with traditional coding skills. These tasks may not be able to provide a high level of clarity that traditional coding need, or they have too much in terms of complexity that comes with them.

You will find that the first category of tasks that we are going to look at here is going to be any that a person or some kind of animal would be able to perform. For example, speech recognition, driving, and even image recognition would fit into here. Humans are able to do this without even thinking, but they would be really hard to teach a program to work with, especially if you are trying to use some conventional coding techniques. But machine learning will be able to step in and make sure that this works out the way that you would like.

The next issue that you may run into when working with the idea of machine learning is that it is going to handle some tasks and concepts that a human could run into some trouble. This may include doing things like going through huge amounts of data or at least a complex type of data. There are many companies who collect data about their customers to use in the future. But if the company is big, that is a ton of data to work with.

While a person would be able to do this and maybe come up with a decent analysis, it would take forever. And by the time they got all of that data sorted through, there would probably be new data that needs some attention, and they would fall behind and be using outdated information. With machine learning, the business would be able to go through this information quickly and come up with some smart predictions that would be easy to use and promote the business forward.

You may find that you can use some of the concepts that come with machine learning to help with projects that work with genomic data, weather prediction, and search engines. There is going to be a lot of information that is seen as valuable with all of the different sets of data, but it is hard to find the time and the energy to go through this information. And it may not be done in a manner that is timely. But machine learning can step in and get it done.

If you have already spent some time learning about traditional programming and you know how to use a traditional coding language, then it is likely that you already know some of the cool things that you are able to do with them. But there are a lot of different things and things that will be more useful as technology progresses even more that machine learning will be able to help you to do.

Adaptively Generated Tasks

You will find that conventional programs can do a lot of really cool things, but there are some limitations to watch out for. One of these limitations is that these conventional programs are a little bit rigid. Once you write out the code and implement it, the codes are going to stay the same all the time. These codes will do the same thing over and over unless the programmer changes the code, but they can't learn and adapt.

There will be times when you are working on a program that you want to act in a different manner or react to an input that it receives. Working with a conventional program will not allow this to happen. But working with machine learning allows you to work with a method that teaches the program how to change. Spam detection in your email showed a good example of how this can work.

Machine learning is easier to work with than you would think.

Yes, there are going to be some algorithms and other tasks that come with machine learning that are more complex and take some time to learn. There are a lot of examples of what is possible with machine learning that is actually pretty simple. Your projects are going to be more complicated compared to what you saw with regular programming, but machine learning is able to take those complicated tasks and make them easier. You will be surprised at how easy it is to use the programming techniques of machine learning to do some tasks like facial recognition and speech recognition.

Machine learning is often the choice to work with because it has the unique ability to learn as it goes along the process. For example, we are able to see how this works with speech recognition. Have you ever used your smartphone or another device to talk to it and had some trouble with it being able to understand you, especially in the beginning? Over time, though, the more that you were able to use the program, the better it got at being able to understand you. In the beginning, you may have had to repeat yourself over and over again, but in the end, you are able to use it any way that you would like and it will understand you. This is an example of how machine learning is able to learn your speech patterns and understand what you are saying over time.

While machine learning is going to be able to work with a lot of different actions that may be considered complex, you will find that it is really easy to work with some of the codes that go with it and you may be surprised at how a little coding can go a long way. If you have already worked with a bit of coding and programming in the past, then you will be able to catch on quick, and it won't take much longer for those who are brand new to the idea either.

What are some of the ways that I can apply machine learning?

Now that we know a bit more about the different benefits that come with machine learning, it is time to move on and learn a bit more about some of the other things that you are going to be able to do with this as well. As you start to work with the process of machine learning a bit more, you will find that there are a lot of different ways that you are able to use it and many programmers are taking it to the next level to create things that are unique and quite fun.

You may also start to notice that there are many different companies, from startups to more established firms, that are working with machine learning because they love what it is able to do to help their business grow. There are so many options when it comes to working with machine learning, but some of the ones that you may use the most often are going to include:

- Statistical research: machine learning is a big part of IT now. You will find that machine learning will help you to go through a lot of complexity when looking through large data patterns. Some of the options that will use statistical research include search engines, credit cards, and filtering spam messages.

- Big data analysis: many companies need to be able to get through a lot of data in a short amount of time. They use this data to recognize how their customers spend money and even to make decisions and predictions about the future. This used to take a long time to have someone sit through and look at the data, but now machine learning can do the process faster and much more efficiently. Options like election campaigns, medical fields, and retail stores have used machine learning for this purpose.

- Finances: some finance companies have also used machine learning. Stock trading online has seen a rise in the use of machine learning to help make efficient and safe decisions and so much more.

As we have mentioned above, these are just three of the ways that you are able to apply the principles of machine learning in order to get the results that you want to aid in your business or even to help you create a brand new program that works the way that you want. As technology begins to progress, even more, you will find that new applications and ideas for how this should work are going to grow as well.

Are there certain programs I can use machine learning with?

By now, you shouldn't be too surprised that there are a lot of different programs that you are able to utilize with machine learning, and many more are likely to be developed as time goes on. This makes it a really fun thing to learn how to work with and your options are pretty much going to be limited only by your imagination and coding skills.

There are a lot of different applications where you are able to use machine learning, and you will find that each of them can show you a different way that machine learning is going to work. Some examples of what you are able to do when you start to bring out machine learning will include:

• Search engines: A really good example of machine learning is with search engines. A search engine is going to be able to learn from the results that you push when you do a search. The first few times, it may not be as accurate because there are so many options, and you may end up picking an option that is further down the page. But as you do more searches, the program will learn what your preferences are and it can get better at presenting you with the choices that you want.

www.ingramcontent.com/pod-product-compliance
Lightning Source LLC
LaVergne TN
LVHW022315060326
832902LV00020B/3470